A PRIMER OF NEWSPAPER CHINESE

Yu-Ju Chih

with the assistance of
John S. Montanaro

讀報入門

YALE UNIVERSITY
NEW HAVEN, CONNECTICUT

FOREWORD

In the teaching of many languages - particularly those of the Western world - it may be assumed that the ability to read a newspaper follows automatically after a certain amount of practice in general elementary reading. In Chinese, however, there has been and still is a marked difference between the purely spoken style and the so-called newspaper style, the latter tending toward the classical literary style in its conventionality and compactness. It is true that since the second decade of this century there has been an increasing demand in China for the printing of news written entirely in the colloquial style. And ,with the advent of Communist rule in China, the response to this demand has been very positive, although one still finds many of the conventions of the literary language still present in their publications. In any case, Chinese newspapers published in Taiwan or in Hong Kong or those published for overseas Chinese readers still strongly retain the traditional newspaper style. Students of Chinese in countries outside of China will often be exposed to and have easier access to this kind of newspaper. Moreover it is precisely this written newspaper style with its literary conventions that offers excellent training for eventual reading of modern prose of all sorts.

The annotated selections from Chinese newspapers contained in this book have gone through several years of revision and classroom testing in the classrooms of Yale University where an introduction to newspaper reading begins in late second year (intensive) and continues during the student's third year (non-intensive). Naturally, in a book of this sort, the specific content of the articles becomes out of date soon after publication. But users will find, we trust, that the general content of the selection topics are still curiously current in today's world. State leaders are still visiting one another, government reports are still being published, nations are still contending, natural calamities are still with us, and so on. The important thing for the student to remember is that this excellent text covers the vast majority of structural patterns commonly met in reading Chinese newspapers or advanced Chinese prose.

After the introductory lesson which introduces certain basic vocabulary items, the selections themselves are taken directly from Chinese newspapers. This text assumes that the user will have command of at least 800 basic Chinese characters (see list, page 189). With a lesser number the user is apt to find that excessive dictionary work to look up items not glossed in the notes will distract him from the main concern, which is sentence structure rather than vocabulary.

This book is a volume in the Mirror Series of Chinese language texts. In this series basic reading skills are taught primarily through the following texts:

Read Chinese, Book One, by Fred Fangyu Wang.
Introduces 300 characters.
Lady in the Painting, by Fred Fangyu Wang,
a review text for the first level.
Read About China, by Pao-chen Lee.
Introduces an additional 300 basic characters
and 100 more not treated as lesson requirement.
Read Chinese, Book Two, by Richard Chang. An
alternative to Read About China. Introduces 300
characters.
Strange Stories from a Chinese Studio, by Roger Yueh. a
review text for the second level.
Read Chinese, Book Three, by Richard Chang and Fred
Wang. Introduces 400 additional characters bringing
total recognition to 1000. Newspaper reading often
begins at this stage.

Many other texts and materials are used as supplements. Complete lists or other advice can by obtained by writing the publisher.

Introduction to the Second Revised Edition

This slightly expanded and revised re-issue of Y. J. Chih's classic introduction to the style, syntax and vocabulary of Chinese newspapers has been prepared and printed chiefly in response to the many requests from teachers of intermediate and higher levels of Chinese. When, after several attempts to completely revise the book failed, it was decided that, rather than tamper with a "classic", we would update a few of the lessons and add few new ones drawn from recent Chinese newspapers. With Professor Chih's agreement, I updated the first two lessons, eliminated lessons fourteen through eighteen of the original edition, and added selections seventeen through twenty-six of the present volume. Of these new additions, selections seventeen and eighteen had been previously annotated by Professor Chih in an earlier edition of the book, while the remaining added selections, from twenty through twenty-six, were chosen and annotated by me. I also completely revised the vocabulary index to accord with the new content. Both of us hope that this modest revision of this most useful volume will add additional years to the life of the book and benefit students seeking to gain training in how to read Chinese newspapers and other forms of advanced prose.

John Montanaro
Yale University
January, 1987

ACKNOWLEDGEMENTS

It is with deep gratitude that I acknowledge the help received from many of my colleagues on the staff of the Institute of Far Eastern Languagees during the preparation of this book.

I am particulary indebted to Mr. Henry C. Fenn for his sustained interest, encouragement and advice throughout the project, and specifically for his contribution of the structural graphs which appear in the notes. Professor George Kennedy also has given much time and thought to the content and form of the text and his suggestions have benefited me greatly. Thanks are also expressed to Miss Alice Wan for her assistance and untiring patience in proofreading and compilation; to Mrs. Gloria Hsia for typing the entire manuscript; to Mrs. Mulien Wu and Mrs. Sum Wai Wang for writing the Chinese characters in the texts and notes; and to Miss Ida Tyrrell and Mrs. Sophia O'Neill for their important help.

The idea of writing the Introduction (which is not a newspaper article but rather a simplified introduction to newspaper reading) is based on a book published by the Chinese department of the Army Language School at the Presidio of Monterey, California.

Yu-Ju Chih

TABLE OF CONTENTS

INTRODUCTION

News, News Agencies and Newspapers

新聞·通訊社·報紙

甚麼是「新聞」？「新」就是新鮮或是新奇；「聞」是見聞的意思。看見的或聽見的新奇事情就叫新聞。比方說，狗咬了人，這是很平常的事，不能說是新聞。但是，如果人咬了狗，那就是新聞了。

新鮮或新奇的事常有不同的新聞價值；有的事情新聞價值大，有的事情新聞價值小。一件事情的新聞價值常常因人、因地、因時、就不一樣。例如，張三明天要到英國去、也許沒有新聞價值；但是，美國總統如果明天到英國去，也許新聞價值很大。五十年前在美國發生的事，在今天的日本有沒有新聞價值、或新聞價值有多麼大，那就很難說了。

一件新聞發生以後，有的時候報館派記者去「採訪」，然後登在他們的報上；但是平常都是通訊社把這個新聞打聽清楚，再給報館。

世界上有很多有名的大通訊社。中國的新

華社、中華民國(臺灣)的中央社、美國的美聯社和合眾國際社，天天在報上可以看到。英國最出名的通訊社叫路透社。蘇聯有塔斯社。

現在談到報紙。報紙有的是政黨辦的，有的是教會或私人辦的。報紙的立場和觀點常常可以從他們的社論裏、他們的新聞編排上、甚至於他們所登的廣告裏看出來。

VOCABULARY A - NEW CHARACTERS

(Characters of less importance are starred. This practice will be followed throughout the book.)

1. 訊	syìn (or syùn)	N:	news, information
通訊	tūngsyìn	VO:	communicate by letter
		N:	communication by letter or telegram
通訊處	tūngsyìnchù	N:	mailing address
通訊社	tūngsyìnshè	N:	news agency (See Voc. B-11)
2. 咬	yǎu	V:	bite, gnaw
3. 者	-jě	BF:	one (that), those (who or which) - added to a verb to indicate one who does the act. Equivalent of -<u>de rén</u> or <u>de</u> + N (usually understood) in colloquial Chinese
大者	dàjě	N:	large one
到會者	dàu-hwèije	N:	those who attend the meeting

Furthermore, it appears in a number of fixed expressions:

記者	jìjě	N:	news reporter
學者	sywéjě	N:	scholar
讀者	dújě	N:	reader (person)
4. 登	dēng	V:	publish (also; ascend, mount)

	登報	dēngbàu	VO: publish in a newspaper
	登記	dēngjì	V/N: register/registration
5.	蘇	sū	N: (a common surname. The character is used to transliterate foreign names)
	蘇聯	Sūlyán	N: Soviet Union
6.	編	byān	V: edit
	編排	byānpái	V/N: edit/editing
	編者	byānjě	N: editor (literary)
7.	私	sz̄	BF: private (as opposed to "public")
	私人	sz̄rén	N: private individual
8.	場	chǎng	N: field, flat area
	立場	lìchǎng	N: position, standpoint
9.	廣	gwǎng	SV: broad, wide
	廣告	gwǎnggàu	N: advertisement, notice

Vocabulary B - New Expressions and Structural Analysis

1. 報(紙)	bàu(jř)	N:	newspaper
日報	r̀bàu	N:	daily (newspaper)
晚報	wǎnbàu	N:	evening paper
2. 報館	bàugwǎn	N:	newspaper (office)
3. 見聞	jyànwén	N:	observation, experience (lit. things seen or heard)
4. 如果	rúgwǒ	MA:	if
5. 因人	yīn rén...		Yīn stands for yīnwei, "because" "on account of"
6. 例如	lìrú	IE:	for example
7. 張三	Jāng Sān	N:	a fictitious name
8. 總統	dzǔngtǔng	N:	president (of a government)
9. 採訪	tsǎifǎng	V:	cover; gather (news)
10. 然後	ránhòu	MA:	afterwards, then
11. 中央(通訊)社	Jūngyāng (tūngsyìn)shè	N:	Central News Agency (Kuomintang)
新華社	Syīnhwáshè	N:	New China Agency
美聯社	Měilyánshè	N:	Associated Press (Sometimes known as 聯合社 Lyánhéshe)

合衆國際社	Héjùng Gwójìshè	N: United Press International
路透社	Lùtòushè	N: Reuters
塔斯社	Tǎszshè	N: Tass
12. 政黨	jèngdǎng	N: political party
13. 觀點	gwāndyǎn	N: point of view
14. 社論	shèlwùn	N: editorial
15. 甚至於	shènjìryu	A: even, to the point of

16. 所 + V ... de

所 <u>swǒ</u> plus a verb is usually translated into a relative clause in English introduced by 'who' or 'that which'. Such a clause when followed by the colloquial particle 的 <u>-de</u> or its literary equivalent 之 <u>-jr̄</u> may modify the following noun.

所登的廣告 swǒ dēngde gwǎnggàu - the advertisement which is inserted.

NOTES

1. This Introductory Lesson is not a selection from a Chinese newspaper. It is a reading exercise made to introduce certain terms commonly used in newspaper work.

2. Literary and semi-literary expressions play a much larger part in news writing than in <u>báihwa</u> (colloquial) literature. Literary forms are more compact, and space-saving is an economic consideration for the publisher. Communist newspapers tend to use a style closer to <u>báihwa</u> than non-Communist publications,

doubtless in an effort to reach the masses.

3. Punctuation. The punctuation marks used in modern Chinese writing were for the most part borrowed from occidental languages; in general, western usage is followed. An exception is the use of a half-comma (、) to separate listed items. Note its use in the second paragraph of this lesson.

EXERCISES

INTRODUCTION

1. 美國兩個最大的通訊社,一個是美聯社,一個叫合眾國際社。這兩個通訊社平常派記者到世界各地去"採訪"新聞。

2. 中央社是中國國民黨辦的,代表中國政府的立場。據說,中央社現在有三位記者在美國,一位在法國。

3. 新華社是中國共產黨的通訊社,代表中國共產黨政府的立場。美國報紙不但用中央社的新聞,也登新華社所發的消息。

4. 路透社有很久的歷史,平常代表英國政府的觀點。

5. 塔斯社是蘇聯的通訊社,據說,蘇聯只有這一個通訊社。

6. 美國有兩個大的政黨,一個叫民主黨,一個叫共和黨。這兩個政黨常常有不同的觀點。

7. 他天天看報。他不但看報上的新聞,也愛讀社論.有的時候,連報上的廣告都看。

8. 張先生是一個新聞記者.他每天早上八點鐘到報館去,下午五點半回家.

9. 那個城裏有五家報紙.一家是教會辦的,别的都是私人辦的.

10. 有人說,愛大聲叫的狗不咬人。

11. 每日新聞 (DAILY NEWS) 有很多讀者.這個報紙常登好看的像片,讀者們喜歡看.

12. 新聞價值大的新聞登在報紙的第一頁.新聞價值小者登在第十頁.

SELECTION 1

Census of Chinese People's Republic Completed

中國第三次人口調查登記

最後統計數字正式公佈

今年七月全國人口十億三千一百八十餘萬

紐約時報二日載北京專電：以今年七月一日為準的中國第三次全國人口調查登記，最後結果已正式公佈。

北京電台一日廣播中華人民共和國國家統計局關於全國人口調查

登記結果的公報。公報說，中國全國人口總數，在一九八二年七月三十日，是十億三千一百八十八萬二千五百一十一人。這個總數包括台灣省人口一千八百二十七萬零七百四十九人。總數字並包括海外華僑一千一百七十四萬三千三百二十人。

（紐約華僑日報一九八二年十一月三日）

VOCABULARY A - NEW CHARACTERS

1. 調	dyàu	BF: V:	investigate transfer, move
調查	dyàuchá	V/N:	investigate investigation
2. 佈	bù	V:	spread, inform
公佈	gūngbù	V:	make public
佈告	bùgàu	V/N:	announce announcement
3. 億	yì	NU:	100,000,000
4. 載	dzài	V:	record, carry
記載	jìdzài	V:	record in history
5. 港	gǎng	N:	a port, harbor
港口	gǎngkǒu	N:	a port
商港	shānggǎng	N:	a commercial port
香港	Syānggǎng	PW:	Hongkong
6. 台(臺)	tái	N:	terrace, platform
電台	dyàntái	N:	radio station
7. 播	bwō (bwò)	V:	sow, disseminate
廣播	gwǎngbwō	V:	broadcast (radio)
播音	bwōyīn	VO:	go on the air (radio)
8. 括	kwò	BF:	include, comprise
包括	bāukwò	V:	include

括號	kwòhàu	N: parentheses
9. 灣	wān	N: a bay, bend of a stream
台灣	Táiwān	PW: Taiwan (Formosa)
海灣	hǎiwān	N: gulf, bay
10. 僑	chyáu	V: lodge, sojourn
華僑	hwáchyáu	N: overseas Chinese
外僑	wàichyáu	N: foreign nationals
僑民	chyáumín	N: foreign nationals

Vocabulary B - New Expressions and Structural Analysis

1. 人口	rénkǒu	N: population

Note that this compound is made up with a N (noun) plus its own M (measure) following it, and thus it assumes either a collective or an abstract sense of the N.

Similar expressions include:

(wǔ)lyàngchē 五輛車 -- chēlyàng 車輛 (vehicles)

(wǔ)jāngjř 五張紙 -- jřjāng 紙張 (paper, in the collective sense

(wǔ)jīchwán 五隻船 -- chwánjī 船隻 (ships, as such)

(wǔ)jīchyāng 五枝鎗 -- chyāngjī 鎗枝 (rifles)

2. 人口調查登記	rénkǒu dyàuchá dēngjì	N:	census (population)
3. 統計	tǔngji	N:	counting, statistics
國家統計局	Gwójyā Tǔngjì Jyú	N:	State Statistics Board
4. 數字	shùdz	N:	figure, number
總數(字)	dzǔngshù(dž)	N:	total figure
5. 餘	yú	NU:	and plus, -odd <u>yú</u> is a suffix to a NU, similar to the colloq. dwō. (In literary Chinese, it is sometimes preceded by <u>yoǔ</u>.)
6. 紐約	Nyǒuywē	PW:	New York
紐約時報	Nyǒuywēshŕbàu	N:	<u>The New York Times</u>
7. 電	dyàn	N:	cable, (telegraphic) dispatch
8. 以……為……	yǐ...wéi...CV...V...:		to take ...to be..., to consider as

This is a case of two verbal expressions in a series in which the two verbs go hand in hand. <u>Yǐ</u> means "to take" corresponding to the colloq. <u>ná</u> ;<u>wéi</u>, "to be" or "as".

The pattern can be either yǐ N + wéi N, or yǐ N + wéi SV.

以…為準 yǐ...wéi jwǔn — to take ... as the basis

8. 以…為…的 yǐ...wéi...de + N

This is a case of a N modified by a substantive clause. The key is de from which the student should make a practice of tracing back in order to determine the beginning of the modifier.

9. 已 yǐ — A: already (literary abbrev. for yǐjing)

10. 正式 jèngshr̀ — SV/A: formal/officially (the opposite is 非正式 fēijèngshr̀)

11. Remark on the first paragraph.
Note that the structure of the first paragraph is:
S (subject) ---- S (subject) ---- P (predicate)
rénkǒu dyàuchá dēngjì   dzwèihòu jyégwǒ   gūngbù
There are at least two possible interpretations for the above sentence pattern:
(1) To take the first S as a pre-stated topic and the second S as the subject of the sentence. Thus:
As to ... census, the final result ...
(2) To take the first S as a noun modifying the second S which is the subject of the sentence. Thus:
The final result of (such a) census ...

12. 北京	Běijīng	PW:	Peking
13. 一日	yíř	NU- N:	the first day (of the month); one day

yíř means either "(on) the first day of the month: or "one day". This ambiguity may be removed if the month is mentioned.

For instance, 三月十日 Sānywe shŕr, "the tenth of March".
On the other hand, 一天 yityān simply means "one day".

14. 中華人民共和國	Jūnghwá Rénmín Gùnghégwó	N:	Chinese People's Republic
中華	Jūnghwá	N:	the Chinese (as a nation)
共和國	gunghégwó	N:	a republic
15. 關於	gwānyu	CV:	concerning, with respect to
16. 公報	gūngbàu	N:	bulletin

17. 北京電台……廣播……公報 Subject...V...Object

This is the first sentence in the second paragraph of the news story.

It may be translated as "The Peking radio broadcast on the first a bulletin (of the National Board of Statistics of the People's Republic of China) on (or concerning) the result of a nation-wide census." In the Chinese text "gwānyu...de" constitute a modifier modifying gūngbàu which stands immediately after de. Hence, de is the key word in this pattern; it winds up a modifying phrase or clause.

18. 並	bìng	A: moreover, (abbr. for <u>bìngchyě</u>)
19. 海外	hǎiwài	N: overseas
20. ⋯人	...rén	

Note the absence of <u>gè</u> in front of <u>rén</u>. In newspapers as well as in literary Chinese, the M (measure) is usually left out in NU (number) -M-N (noun).

NOTES

1. Since the headline is pithy and more condensed, it is sometimes advisable to read it after the news story.

2. Note that the first sentence usually points out the main theme of a news story. Subsequent materials fill in the pertinent details. This selection serves as a good example.

3. The Chinese way of counting pauses at wàn (ten thousand) while the Western way pauses at chyān (thousand).

In Chinese, one pauses at wàn, and wàn wàn is called yì. Between the two lie shŕwan, bǎiwan (million) and chyānwan.

1,000,000 (Western)

1,0000,0000 (Chinese)

百萬　千

4. 華僑日報 China Daily News, from which the present Selection was extracted.

EXERCISES

I. Translate the following into English:

1. 五百萬六千　　2. 一百五十萬餘人
3. 一億六千二百萬多人

II. Render the following figures into Chinese:

1. 26,500　　2. 878,101　　3. 32,554,399

III. Translate the following into English:

1. 以去為好　　2. 以回國為理由
3. 以上海為中心

IV: Translate:

1. 這個報廣告太多.　(Note the S-S-P structure)
2. 那件事結果很好.　(Note the S-S-P structure)
3. 那個電台每天廣播五次新聞.
4. 港口裏有很多船隻.
5. 台灣現在有美國僑民四千餘人.

EXERCISES-SELECTION I

1. 紐約時報在紐約城裏。紐約時報不但登載美國國內新聞，國外新聞也非常詳細。

2. 美國每十年調查登記一次人口。一九五〇年，美國有一億六千萬人。一九八〇年，美國人口總數為二億兩千六百萬人。

3. 美國一九八〇年的人口調查登記，以四月一日為準。

4. 紐約是美國最大的城。人口有多少，我不知道。聽說有七百餘萬人。

5. 一九八二年，中國共產黨政府調查登記一次人口。人口調查登記的結果，國家統計局已經公佈。

6. 一九五三年中國人口總數是六億零一百萬人。這個數字包括台灣人口和海外華僑。

7. 英國人口有六千萬人。日本的人口，據一九八六年的統計，有一億一千九百萬人。

8. 那個新聞，今天不但報紙登載出來，電台也廣播了。

9. 香港是一個商港,不是一個軍港。五十餘年以前,香港只是一個小城。現在人口已經有四百多萬.

10. 據政府的公報,台灣的人口已有兩千萬.

11. 住在美國的外國僑民,每年一月裏應當向美國政府登記。外僑的總數,美國政府一定有統計.

12. 這個數字不是正式的數字。正式的數字,政府還没公佈。

SELECTION 2

China's Centenarians Total Over 3,700

中國百歲以上老人
共有三千七百餘名

（紐約時報 十一月一日香港電）北京電台宣佈，中國人口共有十億三千一百餘萬，其中包括臺灣人口及香港和澳門地區的人口。

中國大陸之人口確數為十億零八百一十七萬五千三百二十八人。大城市人口，上海有一千一百八十五萬九千七百四十八人，北京有九百二十三萬零六百八十七人。

全國人口以性別而分，男性佔百分之五十一點五。以年齡而分，百分之五十三點九二在十九歲以上。以種族而分，百分之九十點三為漢人。全國年齡在一百歲以上之老人，共有三千七百六十五名。東北三省人口為九千零九十四萬七千三百九十二人。四川為人口最多之省份，共有九千九百七十一萬三千三百一十人。

（紐約聯合日報 一九八二年十一月三日）

Vocabulary A - New Characters

1. 宣		sywān	BF: proclaim
	宣佈	sywānbù	V: proclaim, announce (officially)
2. 及		jí	CV: and, together with (lit.)
	以及	yị̌jí	CV: and
3. 陸		lù	N: land
	陸地	lùdì	N: dry land
	大陸	dàlù	N: mainland, continent
	陸軍	lùjyūn	N: ground forces, army
4. 確		chywè	SV/A: precise, reliable, verily
	確實	chywèshŕ	SV/A: reliable, truthfully
	的確	dìchywè	MA: really, indeed
	確數	chywèshù	N: exact figure
5. 齡		líng	BF: age
	年齡	nyánlíng	N: age
6. 族		dzú	N: clan, race
	種族	jǔngdzú	N: race
	民族	míndzú	N: nation, people
7. 漢		Hàn	N: Hans Chinese (as opposed to minority peoples in China)
8. 川		chwān	N: stream, riverlet

四川 Sżchwān PW: Szechwan Province

9. 份 fèn M: portion, share (cf. Voc. B-10)

Vocabulary B - New Expressions and Structural Analysis

1. 北京 Běijīng PW: Peking

2. 其 chí PN: his, their, its/that

(1) As an adjunct, with an antecedent previously stated.

其中 chíjūng -- in which, in that

其上 chíshàng --on which, above or over that

(2) As a possessive pronoun of the third person, followed by a N:

其書 chí shū -- his (her) book

其人 chí rén -- that person

(3) It occurs in a number of fixed expressions:

其實 chíshŕ Ph: as a matter of fact

其餘 chíyú SP: the rest (of it)

3. 為 wéi V: to be (is, was, am, are, etc.)

4. 城市 chéngshr̀ N: cities

5. 而 ér CV/A: and, and yet/however, yet

(1) Ér is an adjunct adverb in literary Chinese typically used to link two verbal expressions or two clauses in juxtaposition. E.g.

gāu ér dà 高而大 — be tall and large

Jyà lyán ér wù měi 價廉而物美 — The price is low and the thing is good.

(2) Ér may be used to link either two verbal expressions, or one adverbal expression and one verb, or two clauses which are not coordinates but with the second predominating or taking place under the circumstances or in the manner described by the first. E.g.

syǎu ér jùng 小而重 — be small and yet heavy

Jyà lyán ér wù bùměi 價廉而物不美 — The price is low and the thing no good.

yínù ér chyù 一怒而去 — to go away in anger

sywán ér wèi jywé 懸而未決 — pending and was not decided upon

(3) Ér assumes the meaning of " to " or " to become "

when it goes with CV, such as tsúng or the like.

yóu syǎu ér dà 由 小 而 大	from small (change) to big

(4) Er is usually optional when preceded by an adverbial phrase (with a CV in it) and followed by a V.

wèi héping (ér) nǔlì 為 和平(而)努力	to work earnestly for peace

In this case, wèi is a CV and nǔlì, a V.

yǐ...ér fēn 以…而 分	to distinguish by (or on the basis of) ...

"yǐ...fēn" forms a chain of verbal expressions which go hand in hand. Yǐ means "to take"; fēn, "to distinguish" or "to divide". Yǐ is a CV and fēn, a V; therefore ér may be left out.

6. 之 jr̄ Particle: of, 's (corresponding to the possessive de in spoken Chinese) PN: him, it, them (a generalized object)

Jr̄ has five major uses:

(1) Used in the standard formula for fractions:

$$\frac{X}{Y} = \text{Y-fēnjr̄-X}$$

E.g.

五分之一 wǔfēnjr̄yī	one-fifth
百分之… bǎifēnjr̄...	...per cent

(2) As a possessive particle. The pattern is N + jr̄ + N; in this case, jr̄ is interchangeable with the colloq. de. E.g.

我之書	wǒ jr̄ shū	my book
張先生之母	Jāng Ss. jr̄ mǔ	Mr. Chang's mother

(3) Jr̄ with a character like chyán, hòu, jūng, or dūng, etc. forms a localizer, used after a time-word or a place-word. e.g.

…之前	...jr̄chyán	before...,ago; in front of... (cf. yichyán)
…之中	...jr̄jūng	in the middle of..., amid...
…之外	...jr̄wài	outside..., apart from ...(cf. yǐwài)
…之東	...jr̄dūng	east of...(yǐdūng)

(4) Jr̄ + SV has the meaning of "as SV as" E.g.

五年之久	wǔnyán jr̄ jyǒu	as long as five years

(5) Jr̄ may be used in literary Chinese as a pronoun, third person, either singular or plural in number, but in objective case.

吃之	chr̄ jr̄	to eat it
置之不理	jr̀ jr̄ bù lǐ	disregard it (put it aside and disregard it)

It goes without saying that jr̄, in this case, is preceded by a verb.

7. 性別	syìngbyé	N: sex (to distinguish male from female)
男性	nánsyìng	N: male, men

女性	nyǔsyìng	N: female, women
8.····以上	...yǐshàng	above..., more than..

yǐ is often joined by localizers or time expressions:

...以東...	yǐdūng	to the east of ...
...以內...	yǐnèi	within ...
...以外...	yǐwài	outside of, except ...
...(以)前...	yǐchyán	formerly, before....
...(以)來...	yǐlái	since...,for the past ...
9. 名	míng	M: for persons
10. 省份	shěngfèn	N: province (as an administrative division)

Note that shěng means "province" in the concrete sense but when fèn is attached to it, it tends to be abstract, meaning "province" as an administrative division. Similar expressions include:

縣份	syànfèn	N: county (as such)
月份	ywèfèn	N: month
五月份	wǔywèfèn	N: the month of May (as a monthly division)

NOTES

1. This selection is obviously based on the same material as Selection 1.

   聯合日報 The United Journal, from which this Selection was taken, is an independent paper in New York City. It seems to have treated this news item rather lightly because the headline it chooses here suggests that it is more interested in the number of centenarians than in all the figures of the census undertaken by the Communist regime.

2. In Chinese newspapers the source is always stated at the beginning of a new story, as evidenced here in Běijīng Dyàntái Sywānbù. Similar expressions include:

東京消息	Dūngjīng syāusyi	News dispatch from Tokyo
香港二十日訊	Syānggǎng èrshr-shr̀ syìn	News dated the 20th from Hong-Kong
上海二日電	Shànghǎi èr̀r dyàn	Cable of the 2nd from Shanghai
台北廣播訊	Táiběi gwǎngbwō syìn	Broadcast from Taipeh
香港航訊	Syānggǎng háng syìn	Dispatch from Hongkong via air mail

3. Major peoples in China

漢(族)	Hàn(dzú)	N: Hans (bulk of the Chinese people)
滿	Mǎn	N: Manchus (practically assimilated by the Hans at the downfall

		of the Ching or Manchu Dynasty)
蒙	Méng	N: Mongolians
回	Hwéi	N: Mohammedans
藏	Dzàng	N: Tibetans

Important minority peoples include:

苗	Myáu	N: Miaos (scattered in the SW)
僮	Jwàng	N: Chuang nationality (in SW China)

EXERCISES

1. Translate into English the following phrases (or clauses) with ér.

1. 自遠而近 2. 低飛而過
3. 因這個原因而調查 4. 從英國而法國而德國
5. "顯而易見"
6. 他願去,而我不願去.

II. Translate into English:

1. 五十人以上 2. 四十年以前
3. 二十年以來 4. 自他到北京以來
5. 以上所說者,全是真的.

III. Translate into English the following phrases with jr:

1. 北京之西 2. 八月五日之後
3. 公佈之前;公佈之後. 4. 主要問題之一
5. 六萬五十人之多 6. 中國之人口
7. 除李先生之外 8 五百英里之遠

EXERCISES: SELECTION II

1. 下面是一張中文的表,請你念一念.也許你願意填一填.

姓名	
性別	
年歲	
通訊處	

2. 全世界人口共有四十餘億.中國人口有十億之多,佔全世界人口總數的四分之一.

3. 中國人口中,漢人最多,佔百分之九十四.其餘都是少數民族 (MINORITY PEOPLES).

4. 中國的少數民族,以僮族為最大.僮族差不多都住在中國之西南部.他們有他們自己之文字.

5. 世界上所有之人民,不分 (BÙFĒN, REGARDLESS OF) 種族,不分性別,不分宗教,都應當平等.

6. 美國政府宣佈,年齡二十一歲以上者,可以選舉.二十一歲以下者,不能選舉.

7. 香港十八日訊:四川省為中國人口最多之省份,共有九千餘萬人.

8. 美國一九六〇年人口確數已經正式公佈,共有人口一億七千九百六十六萬人,比十年以前多百分之十八點六.一九五〇年,美國有一億五千零六十九萬七千人.

9. 按照人口調查的結果,紐約是美國最大的城.一九六〇年,紐約城的人口為七百七十八萬人.

10. 按照美國人口調查的數字,人口在十萬人以上之城市,一九八〇年有一百三十個之多;十年之前,只有一百零七個.

SELECTION 3

Burmese Premier Visits China

緬甸總理吳努啓程來我國訪問

（新華社二十九日訊）仰光消息：

應中華人民共和國政府的邀請訪問中國的緬甸總理吳努在十一月二十九日上午七時乘飛機離開仰光，經過河內，前往北京。隨同吳努總理訪問中國的有他的夫人都妙意，最高法院法官、前緬甸駐中國大使吳敏登等。中華人民共和國駐緬甸大使姚仲明夫婦同機陪同前往。

（新華社河內二十九日電）應中華人民共和國政府邀請前往中國訪問的緬甸聯邦政府總理吳努和他的夫人，二十九日中午十二時（越南時間）到達越南民主共和國首都河內。

（人民日報一九五四年十一月三十日）

緬甸總理吳努到達北京

（新華社一日訊）應中華人民共和國政府邀請來我國訪問的緬甸聯邦總理吳努和夫人由我國外交部部長助理兼辦公廳主任王炳南、我國駐緬甸大使姚仲明和緬甸駐我國大使吳拉茂陪同，在一日下午四時三十分乘飛機到達北京。

（北京人民日報一九五四年十二月二日）

Vocabulary A - New Characters

1. 啓	chǐ	V:	open, begin (lit.)
2. 程	chéng	N:	journey, road (lit.)
啓程	chí chéng	VO:	start on a journey
起程	chí chéng	VO:	start on a journey
3. 訪	fǎng	V:	visit
訪問	fǎngwèn	V/N:	visit (in official capacity)
4. 邀	yāu	V:	invite
邀請	yāuchǐng	V/N:	invite (a synonyn compound)/invitation
5. 邦	bāng	N:	a state, country
聯邦	lyánbāng	N/SV:	union, federation, federal
友邦	yǒubāng	N:	friendly nations
6. 乘	chèng	CV:	to ride, mount

This word is used to introduce the means of communication employed, interchangeable with 搭 dā, meaning "to take passage." Further expressions:

乘船去	chèng chwán chyù	to go by boat
乘火車去	chèng hwǒche chyù	to go by train

7. 駐	jù	V:	to lodge, reside, stationed at (cf. 住)
8. 達	dá	V:	arrive at, reach

8. 到達	dàudá	V: arrive at (a synonym compound)
9. 首	shǒu	N: head, chief
首都	shǒudū	N: capital (of a country)
10. 兼	jyān	CV: and concurrently V: hold also the position of
11. 廳	tīng	N: hall
客廳	kètīng	N: parlor
飯廳	fàntīng	N: dining room
辦公廳	bàngūngtīng	N: general office

Vocabulary B - New Expressions and Structural Analysis

1. 緬甸	Myǎndyàn	N: Burma
2. 總理	dzǔnglǐ	N: premier
3. 吳努	Wú Nǔ	N: U Nu (U is an honorific title in Burma)
4. 我	wǒ	extended to mean "our" or "us" in literary Chinese
5. 仰光	Yǎnggwāng	PW: Rangoon (capital of Burma)
6. 應	yìng	CV: respond, in response to
應.....邀請	yìng.... yāuchǐng	at the invitation of....; invited by .....

Since yāuchǐng is a synonym compound, the

above may be worded as:

應……之邀 at the invitation of ....

應……之請 at the invitation of ....

The agent of action here may be left out, and in that case the above will become:

應邀 yìng yāu VO: upon invitation

7. 應中華人民共和國政府的邀請訪問中國的……

Here, again, is a modifying clause ended up with the key word de. cf. Selection I, Voc. B - 8

8. 七時	chī shŕ	N: seven o'clock (shŕ - dyǎnjūng)
9. 使	shř	BF: emissary, envoy
大使	dàshř	N: ambassador
公使	gūngshř	N: minister (diplomacy)
大使館	dàshřgwǎn	N: embassy
公使館	gūngshřgwǎn	N: legation
駐……大使	jù....dàshř	Ph: ambassador to....
10. 河內	Hénèi	PW: Hanoi
11. 往	wǎng	V: go (literary)
前往	chyán wǎng	V: go (away from the speaker)

Compare with 前來 chyán lái, to come

12. 隨同	swéitúng	V: follow, accompany
陪同	péitúng	V: accompany

13. 夫人	fūrén	N: Mrs., Madame, wife
14. 都妙意	Dū Myàu Yì	N: Dau Mya Yee
15. 法	fǎ	N: the law
法院	fǎywàn	N: court
法官	fǎgwān	N: judge
16. 前	chyán	BF: ex-, former
17. 吳敏登	Wú Mǐng Dēng	N: U Myint Thein
18. ……等	...děng	BF: and others, and other...

(1) <u>Děng</u> is a sign of plural for personal pronouns.

彼等	bǐděng	PN: they, them
我等	wǒděng	PN: we, us
吾等	* wǔděng	PN: we, us

(2) <u>Děng</u> assumes the meaning of "and other(s)" when preceded by a N. (or a PW, etc.)

上海等地	Shànghǎi děng dì	Shanghai and other places
王先生等(人)		Mr. Wang and others

(3) 等等 <u>děngděng</u>, a duplication of the above, has the meaning of "and so forth".

19. 姚仲明	Yáu Jùngmíng	N: Yao Chung-ming
20. 同機	túngjī	A: on the same airplane

Similar expressions:

同車	túngchē	A: on the same vehicle (or train)
同船	túngchwán	A: on the same boat

21 越南 Ywènán N: Indochina (Note that the archaic pronunciation of 越 is viet.)

22. 由 yóu CV: by/from

(1) Yóu means "from", interchangeable with dż or the colloq. tsúng.

由北京到仰光	yóu Běijīng dàu Yǎnggwāng	From Peking to Rangoon

(2) Meaning "by", it introduces the agent of action. The pattern is: yóu....V.

由····陪同	yóu....péitúng	accompanied by....
由····贊助	yóu....dzànjù	favored and supported by ....

23. 部 bù N: ministry, department (gov't.)

外交部 wàijyāubù N: Ministry of Foreign Affairs

24. 長 jǎng BF: chief, head

部長	bùjǎng	N: minister (of a Ministry)
校長	syàujǎng	N: president (of a college)
市長	shr̀jǎng	N: mayor

25. 助理	jùlǐ	N: assistant
部長助理	bùjǎng jùlǐ	N: assistant to the minister
26. 主任	jǔrèn	N: director
*27. 王炳南	Wáng Bǐngnán	N: Wang Ping-nan
*28. 吳拉茂	Wū Lā Màu	N: U La Maung

29. Graphic Analysis of a Sentence in Newspaper Style

The last paragraph consists of only one sentence that may be analyzed as follows:

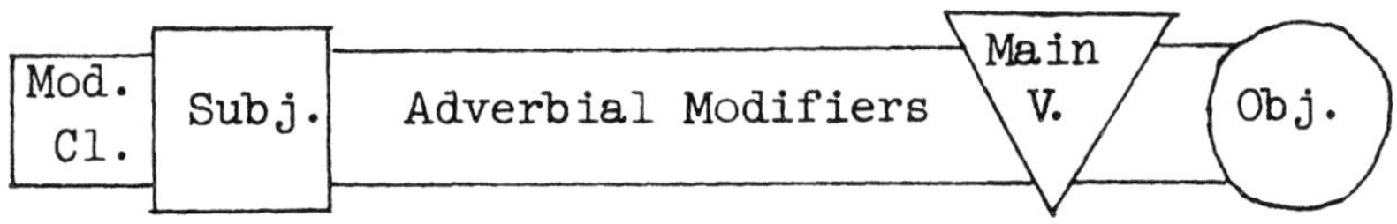

V-Ode	WúNǔ	(CV-O) Accomp.	(CV-O) Time	(CV-O) Means	dàudá	Běijīng
1	2-3-4	5	6	7	8	8

1. yìng...de — N-clause modifying Wú Nǔ

   yìng — main verb of the clause: "respond to"
   Jūng...jèngfǔ — "Chinese People's Republic." This noun modifies yāuchǐng in a possessive sense

   yāuchǐng — N, object of V yìng
   lái...fǎngwèn — purpose expression: "come to pay an official visit"
   de — P, closing the N-clause and indicating that the entire clause modifies some following noun

2. Wú Nǔ — N, subject of the sentence

3. Myǎndyàn dzǔnglǐ — a nominal expression in apposition with Wú Nǔ

4. hé fūren — hé is the equivalent of the colloquial

gēn, which is commonly translated "and". Actually both are CV used in the sense of "together with".

5. yóu...péitúng Coverbial phrase (yóu is a CV and péitúng a verb. Its meaning is "accompanied by". This CV has three objects, the proper names of three persons: Wáng Bìngnán, Yáu Jùngmíng and Wú Lāmàu. cf. this selection Voc. B-22)

6. dzài...fēn Coverbial phrase indicating the time of the action.

7. chèng...fēijī Coverbial phrase indicating the means of transportation.

8. dàudá Main verb followed by its PW object · Běijīng.

The skeleton of a translation would run: "Wú Nǔ, at the invitation of the People's Republic to ..., and his wife, accompanied by 3 persons (named), arrived in Peking at (time), by plane."

NOTES

1. One's official title precedes one's name in Chinese. E.g.

緬甸聯邦總理吳努 U Nu, premier of the Union of Burma

上海市長張一平 Chang Yi-p'ing, mayor of Shanghai

But, a title of address, when used as a description, is usually placed after one's name (or simply one's surname). Thus:

吳努總理 Premier U Nu

張一平市長 Mayor Chang Yi-p'ing
張市長 Mayor Chang

2. News stories involving people traveling usually run like this:

   person---company---time of departure---means of transportation---leaving---by way of---destination---period of stay at the destination.

3. Personal names

   In Chinese, the surname comes first, normally consisting of one character, but occasionally of two characters. The given name has either two characters or one. Consequently, a person's full name has normally three characters, less commonly two or four characters.

   A list of thirty common Chinese surnames may be found in the Appendix of this book. In addition, the student may consult the standard Chinese reference booklet entitled _Pai Chia Hsing_ (_One Hundred Family Names_).

4. To identify a transliterated foreign name is even more difficult. There is no absolute standard as to what characters may be used for sound value only in recording foreign names, but the common usage of the press is slowly crystalizing into such a standard.

   A list of characters commonly employed by the press for transliteration purposes is given in the Appendix.

5. 人民日報, the _People's Daily_, is the most authoritative newspaper of the Chinese Government.

EXERCISES

I. Translate into English

1. 安達北京
2. 達五年之久
3. 上午九時
4. 昨晚十時
5. 前來美國
6. 乘火車前往上海等地
7. 日本駐法大使
8. 仰光美國大使館
9. 法院院長
10. 有紐約市長等人
11. 前美國總統

II. Translate into English

1. 由南到北
2. 由黃河到長江
3. 由上月一日起
4. 由北京啓程
5. 由紐約市長主持
6. 由王市長陪同
7. 由前美國總統代表

III. Translate:

1. 上海市王市長昨天晚上七時三刻乘火車離開上海，前來首都，明天上午八時半可以到達。
2. 前中國駐英大使張大年先生，上月三十日由上海乘船前往日本，同船有華僑四十五人。

SELECTION: III

1. 緬甸聯邦為我國友邦之一。其首都為仰光。

2. 緬甸總理應中華人民共和國之邀請，明天由仰光啓程，飛往北京訪問。隨同前往者有緬甸最高法院院長等人。

3. 我國駐緬甸大使及夫人同機陪同前往。

4. 昨天下午五時我等應邀前往。

5. 南京電：上海市市長兼上海大學校長王正之今日上午八時乘火車前來南京。

6. 我國駐越南大使錢一平夫婦昨天晚上九時半到達北京。

7. 人民日報為中國共產黨所辦之報紙。其社論及新聞之編排代表中國共產黨政府之觀點。

8. 人民日報昨天載有緬甸總理訪問中國之消息。

SELECTION 4

Nehru Warmly Received in Peking

毛主席歡宴尼赫魯總理

（新華社二十三日訊）中華人民共和國毛澤東主席，二十三日晚在中南海歡宴印度共和國總理尼赫魯。

北京各界盛會歡迎尼赫魯總理

據新華社訊：北京市各界人民二十三日下午在中山公園舉行盛大的歡迎會，歡迎應我國政府邀請來我國訪問的印度共和國總理尼赫魯。歡迎大會由北京市市長彭真主持。參加歡迎會的有兩萬多人。

歡迎大會在下午四時四十分開始。尼赫魯總理由周恩來總理和彭真市長陪同，在全場起立鼓掌聲中登上主席台。隨同他們登上主席台的有印度駐我國大使賴嘉文夫婦和隨同尼赫魯總理訪問我國的英廸拉·甘地夫人。

（北京人民日報一九五四年十月二十四日）

VOCABULARY A - NEW CHARACTERS

1. 毛	máu	N: hair/Mao, a surname
2. 席	syí	N: a mat, feast
3 主席	jǔsyí	N: chairman
主席台	jǔsyítái	N: rostrum
出席	chūsyí	V: be present (at a meeting)
3. 宴	yàn	N/V: banquet/to fete
4. 盛(盛)	shèng	SV: abundant, flourishing
盛會	shènghwèi	N/V: a grand meeting/ to hold a grand meeting or rally
盛意	shèngyì	N: (your) generous intentions
5. 持	chŕ	V: grasp, hold, support
主持	jǔchŕ	V: take charge of
支持	jr̄chŕ	V/N: support
保持	bǎuchŕ	V: retain, keep
6. 鼓	gǔ	N: drum
打鼓	dǎ gǔ	VO: drum
7. 掌	jǎng	N: palm
鼓掌	gǔ jǎng	VO: clap the hands, applause

Vocabulary B - New Expressions and Structural Analysis

1. 尼赫魯	Níhèlǔ	N: Nehru
2. 毛澤東	Máu Dzédūng	N: Mao Tse-tung
3. 晚	wǎn	TW: evening (literary abbrev. for wǎnshang)
4. 中南海	Jūng Nán Hǎi	PW: Chung Nan Hai Park
5. 印度	Yìndù	N: India
6. 界	jyè	BF: line of profession
各界	gèjyè	N: all walks of life
學界	sywéjyè	N: educational circles
軍界	jyūnjyè	N: the military
7. 據	jyù	CV: according to

This is one of the commonest and most important characters in Chinese newspapers. It appears in the following patterns:

據……	jyù...V	as...V
據…消息	jyù...syāusyì	according to the news of...
據…宣佈	jyù...sywānbù	as...proclaims, ...proclaims that
據…稱	jyù...chēng	as...asserts, as asserted by
據…指陳	jyù...jřchén	as...points out; as pointed out by...
據…透露	jyù...tòulù	as...discloses
據官方消息	jyù gwānfang syāusyi	according to the

news from official circles

據消息靈通方面稱 jyù syāusyi língtūng fāngmyan chēng
according to well-informed circles

The agent of action in the above patterns may sometimes be left out. Thus:

據稱	jyùchēng	it is asserted that...
據謂	jyùwèi	it is stated that...
據說	jyùshwō	it is said that...

8. 中山公園 Jūngshān Gūngywán PW: Sun Yat-sen Park

9. 舉行 jyǔsyíng V: hold (meeting), convene

10. 會 hwèi N: conference, meeting, parley

開會 kāihwèi VO: hold a meeting

歡迎會 hwānyínghwèi N: welcome party

11. 歡迎應我國政府邀請來我國訪問的印度共和國總理尼赫魯

This is taken from the second paragraph of this Selection.

It means: "to welcome Premier Nehru of India who came to our country for a visit at the invitation of our government". Note de which winds up a clause modifying the N immediately after it.

12. 彭真	Péng Jēn	N:	Péng Chen, name of a person
13. 周恩來	Jōu En-lái	N:	Chou En-lai
14. 起立	chǐlì	V:	stand up (a synonym compound)
15. 在……中	dzài...jūng	PH:	in the midst of..., in the process of...
在進行中	dzài jìnsyíng jūng		in (the process of) progress
在調查中	dzài dyàuchá jūng		in the midst of investigating

Compare the above with the following:

在……内	dzài...nèi	PH:	in, within
在十日内	dzài shŕ̀ nèi		in ten days
在全國内	dzài chywángwó nèi		in the whole country
在可能範圍内	dzài kěnéng fànwéi nèi		within the realm of possibilities

16. 登上	dēngshàng	V:	get onto
17. 賴嘉文	Làijyāwén	N:	Raghaven
18. 甘地	Gāndì	N:	Gandhi
英廸拉甘地	Yǐngdílā Gāndì	N:	Indira Gandhi

EXERCISES

I. Translate into English:

1. 商界 2. 教育界 3. 在辦理中
4. 在計劃中 5. 在其講演中
6. 在建設中 7. 在六個月内

II. Translate into English:

1. 據合衆社訊
2. 據路透社十五日消息
3. 據美政府宣稱
4. 據官方透露
5. 據上海市政府公佈
6. 據可靠方面消息稱

III. Translate into English:

1. 昨天大會的主席是一個學界的人，據説他是一個有名的學者.
2. 王校長走後，現在學校裏的事情由張先生主持.
3. 多謝您的盛意.
4. 據北京消息：印度總理尼赫魯今天上午六時半乘飛機回國，昨日北京各界開一盛會歡送.

SELECTION IV

1. 據官方宣佈,印度共和國總理尼赫魯應我國政府之邀請,昨天下午四時乘飛機到達北京。

2. 昨天晚上八時毛澤東主席在中南海歡宴尼赫魯。中南海是北京城内一個有名的公園。

3. 據新華社消息,北京市各界人民今天上午九時在中山公園舉行歡迎大會,歡迎印度總理尼赫魯。

4. 十月五日晚中山公園之歡迎會非常盛大。歡迎會由北京市市長主持。

5. 尼赫魯由周恩來陪同,到達中山公園。彼等到達會場時,全場起立鼓掌。

6. 英廸拉甘地夫人為尼赫魯之女,一九五四年十月隨同其父訪問中國。

7. 中國差不多每一個大城都有一個中山公園。北京城内的中山公園很有名,其中花草很多。

SELECTION 5

The People's Republic Marks Its Fifth Anniversary

首都各界舉行大會
慶祝建國五週年

毛主席等出席大會
赫魯曉夫等貴賓在會上講話

（新華社三十日訊）國慶節前夕——九月三十日晚，首都各界在中南海懷仁堂隆重舉行中華人民共和國建國五週年國慶慶祝大會。

七時十五分，毛澤東主席偕同

朱德副主席、劉少奇委員長、周恩來總理和全國人民代表大會常務委員會副委員長、國務院副總理、最高人民法院院長、最高人民檢察院檢察長、國防委員會副主席，以及應邀參加我國國慶典禮的各國政府代表團的主要貴賓們登上主席台。這時全體起立，暴風雨般的掌聲響徹全場。

在主席台上的貴賓們有：蘇聯代表團團長尼·謝·赫魯曉夫，團員尼·亞·布爾加寧。

慶祝大會由劉少奇委員長主持。大會開始

，樂隊奏起莊嚴的中華人民共和國國歌。

中華人民共和國國務院總理周恩來在會上作了慶祝中華人民共和國建國五週年的講話。他的講話不斷獲得全場熱烈的掌聲。

接着，蘇聯政府代表團團長赫魯曉夫走上講台。這時，全體起立，熱烈鼓掌。赫魯曉夫在會上發表講話，向我國人民祝賀建國五周年。他的講話不斷為掌聲打斷。

出席慶祝大會的共二千多人。

（人民日報一九五四年十月一日）

Vocabulary A - New Characters

1. 慶		chìng	BF: congratulate, celebrate
	國慶	gwóchìng	N: National Holiday
	國慶日	gwóchìngr̀	N: National Holiday
	國慶節	gwóchìngjyé	N: National Holiday
2. 祝		jù	V: wish, pray, praise
	慶祝	chìngjù	V: congratulate, celebrate, observe
3. 周		jōu	N: Chou, a surname/one turn or revolution
	周年	jōunyán	N: anniversary
4. 賓		bīn	BF: guest
	賓客	bīnkè	N: guest
	來賓	láibīn	N: guest
	貴賓	gwèibīn	N: honorable guest
5. 夕		syì (syī)	N: evening (literary)
	前夕	chyánsyì	TW: on the eve of... the night before
6. 偕		syé	V/CV: accompany, take (some one) along, together with
	偕同	syétúng	V/CV: accompany/together with (a synonym compound)

7. 副	fù	BF: vice-, deputy
副市長	fùshrjǎng	N: deputy mayor
副主席	fùjǔsyí	N: vice-chairman
8. 委	wěi	V: commission, depute
委員	wěiywán	N: a committee member, officer deputed
委員會	wěiywánhwèi	N: committee, a commission
委員長	wěiywánjǎng	N: committee chairman
常務委員會	chángwù wěiywánhwèi	N: standing committee
9. 團	twán	N: group
團體	twǎntǐ	N: body, group
代表團	dàibyǎutwán	N: delegation
團長	twánjǎng	N: chief delegate, head of a delegation
團員	twánywán	N: member of a delegation
10. 暴	bàu	BF: violent, cruel
暴風雨	bàufēngyǔ	N: storm
11. 般	bān	N: sort, way, -like
一般...	yìbān	N: alike, like (same as <u>yíyàng</u>)
12. 獲	hwò	V: acquire, obtain
獲得	hwòdé	V: obtain, receive (a synonym compound)

13. 烈	lyè	BF: ardent, fiery
熱烈	rèlyè	SV: warm, ardent
14 隊	dwèi	N: group, band
樂隊	ywèdwèi	N: band (music)
軍隊	jyūndwèi	N: troops
15. 賀	hè	V: congratulate
祝賀	jùhè	V: congratulate
慶賀	chìnghè	V: congratulate
16. 徹	chè	V: penetrate
17. 奏	dzòu	V: play (musical instruments)

Vocabulary B - New Expressions and Structural Analysis

1. 建國	jyàn gwó	VO/N: set up a nation, founding of a nation
2. 赫魯曉夫	Hèlǔsyǎufū	N: Khrushchev
尼謝 赫魯曉夫	Ní syè Hèlǔsyǎufū	N: Nikita S. Khrushchev
3. 講話	jyǎng hwà	VO: give a talk, deliver a speech (cf. jyǎngyǎn)
4. 懷仁堂	Hwáiréntáng	PW: Hall of Benevolence
5. 隆重	lúngjùng	SV/A: impressive (for ceremony, etc.)
6. 朱德	Jū Dé	N: Chu Teh

7. 劉少奇	Lyóu Shàu-chi	N:	Liu Shao-chi
8. 全國人民代表大會	Chywángwó Rénmín Dàibyǎu Dàhwèi	N:	National People's Congress
9. 國務院	Gwówùywàn	N:	State Council
10. 最高人民檢察院	Dzwèigāu Rénmín Jyǎncháywàn	N:	Supreme People's Procuratorate
檢察長	jyǎnchájǎng	N:	procurator-general
11. 國防委員會	Gwófáng Wěiywánhwèi	N:	National Defence Council
國防	gwófáng	N:	national defence
12. 典禮	dyǎnlǐ	N:	ceremony, rite
13. 主要	jǔyàu	SV:	major, essential
14. 全體	chywántǐ	N:	whole, all the people
15. 尼·亞·布爾加寧	Ní Yǎ Bùěrjyāníng	N:	Nikolai A. Bulganin
16. 在····上			on..., onto..., at...
在會上			at the meeting
	The counterpart is:		
在····下			under..., underneath
17. 莊嚴	jwāngyán	SV:	solemn
18. 接着	jyēje	A:	subsequently
19. 講台	jyǎngtái	N:	speaker's platform
20. 為	wéi	CV/V:	by/be
	wèi	CV:	for

(1) Wéi is a coverb introducing the agent of action. The pattern is:

A wéi B V (or RV)
(A was V by B)

wéi Jāng Syānsheng jyè chyù
為張先生借去 borrowed by Mr. Chang

wéi Wǒ jyūn bāuwéi 為我軍包圍 sorrounded by our troops

wéi Fàjyūn dǎ bài 為法軍打敗 defeated by the French troops

Swǒ 所 may be inserted before the V (or RV). Thus:

wéi Fàjyūn swǒ (dǎ)bài
為法軍所(打)敗 defeated by the French troops (cf. be the French troops' "vanquished")

(2) Wéi, as a full-fledged verb, means 'be', interchangeable with shr̀.

Jèige chwán wéi Fàgwo chwán
這個船為法國船 This is a French ship.

Héjùngshé wéi yi Měigwo tūngsyìnshè.
合衆社為一美國通訊社 U.P. is an American news agency.

Tā wéi Měigwo Jèngfǔ (swǒ) pàichyu jě.
他為美國政府(所)派去者 He was sent by the U.S. government.

Cf. Yi...wéi... (Selection 1, Voc. B-8)

(3) Wèi has the meaning of 'for' or 'for the purpose of':

wèi shr̀jye héping nǔlì
為世界和平努力 to work earnestly for world peace

	wèi hé búchyù 為何不去	why (for what) not going
21. 打斷	dǎdwàn	V: disrupt, interrupt
22. 不斷	búdwàn	A: continually, continuously
23. 向	syàng	CV: to, toward

NOTES

This Selection is designed chiefly to provide the student with the important offices and the leading figures of the Communist Government in China, familiarity of which should be helpful to a thorough understanding of Chinese newspapers. A chart of the governmental structure of the People's Republic of China may be found in the Appendix.

EXERCISES

I. Identify:

1.其 2.兼 3.副 4.及 5.以及
6.首都 7.主席 8.廣播 9.國防
10.全體人民

II. Translate the following either into colloquial Chinese or into English:

1. 為他所殺
2. 為英軍殺死
3. 為教會設立者
4. 東京為日本之首都.
5. 他為調查這事而來.
6. 為建設新中國而努力

III. Translate:

1. 祝你一路平安
2. 現在我們全體都站起來,唱美國國歌.
3. 這個委員會有委員十四人.
4. 美國的國慶日是七月四日.每年到了那天,美國全國各地都舉行慶祝會.
5. 北京電:北京市副市長王平遠等人昨天上午八時乘火車前往上海南京等地.

1. 甚麽是"共和國"?共和國裏有一個由人民選舉出來的總統。美國是一個共和國.法國印度都是共和國.蘇聯也是一個大的共和國.

2. 中華人民共和國是一九四九年組成的.全國人民代表大會現在有代表一千二百人.一九五四年九月全國人民代表大會開第一次會的時候,選出毛澤東為中華人民共和國主席,朱德為副主席.一九五九年春天,選出劉少奇為共和國主席.

3. 全國人民代表大會閉會之時,工作由其常務委員會辦理.常務委員會委員長,從一九五四年到一九五九年春天,是劉少奇;一九五九年四月以後,是朱德.

4. 國務院總理,由一九五四年起,一直是周恩來.副總有十餘人.國務院設有很多部,很多委員會.現在,外交部部長為陳毅.

5. 據新華社消息,一九五四年國慶節前夕,首都各界舉行大會,熱烈慶祝我國國慶.

SELECTION 6

Geneva Conference Opens On the 26th

日內瓦會議二十六日開幕

（新華社日內瓦二十六日電）蘇聯、美國、法國、英國、中華人民共和國和其他有關國家參加的日內瓦會議，已在二十六日下午三時在此間國聯大廈開幕。

參加會議的有：中華人民共和國外交部部長周恩來、蘇聯外交部部長莫洛托夫、英國外交大臣艾登、法國外交部部長皮杜爾、美國國務卿杜勒斯、朝鮮民主主義人民共和國外務相南日和大韓民國、澳大利亞、比利時、加拿大、哥倫比亞、阿比西尼亞、希臘、盧森堡、荷蘭、新西蘭、菲律賓、泰國、土耳其等國的代表們。

會議通過由泰國、蘇聯、英國三國代表團首席代表逐日順序輪流擔任會議主席。

擔任第一天會議主席的泰國代表那拉底親王接着致辭。他說，這次會議的召開是為了討論有關亞洲的問題。因此，對亞洲人來說，它是一個最重要的會議。

主席接着並宣讀了瑞士聯邦政府主席給會議的賀電。

在主席宣佈有關會議程序的事項後，會議宣告休會。下次會議將於二十七日下午三時舉行。

（人民日報一九五四年四月二十八日）

Vocabulary A - New Characters

1. 議	yì	V:	discuss
會議	hwèiyì	N:	conference, meeting
全體會議	chwántǐ hwèiyì	N:	plenary session
2. 幕	mù	N:	curtain, screen
開幕	kāi mù	VO:	open (an int. verb for conference, etc.)
3. 臣	chén	N:	officials, courtiers (literary and referring to those as against the monarch in a monarchy.)
大臣	dàchén	N:	minister, high minister
4. 卿	chīng	N:	high minister
國務卿	Gwówùchīng	N:	Secretary of State (U.S.)
5. 逐	jú	BF:	one by one (lit.)
逐日	júr̀	Ph:	day by day
逐漸	jújyàn	A:	little by little, gradually
6. 順	shwùn	V/SV:	follow, obey/convenient, favorable
順利	shwùnlì	SV/A:	smooth, prosperous, smoothly
順便	shwùnbyàn	A:	at one's convenience
7. 序	syù	BF:	series, serial order
次序	tsz̀syù	N:	(serial) order

程序	chéngsyù	N:	sequence, order
8.輪	lwún	V/N:	revolve/a wheel
輪流	lwúnlyóu	A/N:	in rotation/to take turns
9.担(擔)	dān	V:	carry on pole, undertake
担任	dānrèn	V:	undertake, take responsibility
10.致	jr̀	V:	transmit, convey to
致電	jr̀ dyàn	VO:	send a telegram
致賀	jr̀ hè	VO:	convey or extend congratulations
11.辭	tsź	N:	words, expression
致辭	jr̀ tsź	VO:	deliver a speech, speak a few words
12.召	jāu	V:	call, summon
召開	jāukāi	V/N:	to convene/calling (of a meeting)
13.亞	Yǎ	PW:	Asia (abbr. of Yǎjōu)
14.洲	jōu	N:	continent
亞洲	Yǎjōu	PW:	Asia
美洲	Měijōu	PW:	America
非洲	Fēijōu	PW:	Africa
15.它	tā	PN:	it (neutral gender)

16.項	syàng	M:	for things or problems
事項	shr̀syàng	N-M:	matter (in the collective or abstract sense) Cf. Selection 1, Voc. B-1

<u>Vocabulary B</u> - <u>New Expressions and Structural Analysis</u>

1 日内瓦	R̀nèiwǎ	PW:	Geneva
2.其他	chítā	SP:	other (corresponding to the colloq. <u>byéde</u>)
3.有關	yǒugwān	CV/BF:	relate to concerning/related
4.此	tsž̌	SP:	this, here (lit.)
此間	tsž̌jyān	PW:	this place, here (usually referring to the city from which the news item was dispatched)
因此	yīn tsž̌	Ph:	therefore, because of this
此地	tsž̌dì	SP-N:	this place
此後	tsž̌hòu	TW:	after this, hereafter
5.國(際)聯(盟)	Gwó(jì) Lyán(méng)	N:	League of Nations
6.大廈	dàsyà (or shà)	N:	mansion, big hall

7. The first paragraph, consisting of one sentence, may be analyzed graphically as follows:

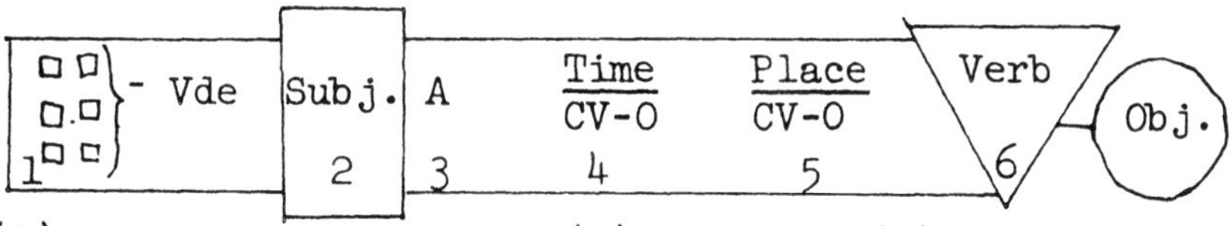

(1)
Sūlyán
Měigwó
Fàgwó
Yīnggwó
Jūnghwá...gwó
chítā...gwójyā
} tsānjyā-de

(2)
Rnèiwǎ
Hweìyì

(3)
yǐ (jìng)

(4)
dzài {26r̀ / syàwǔ / sānshŕ}

(5)
dzài {tsžjyān / Gwólyán Dàsyà}

KAĪ- MÙ

8. 參加會議的(有) tsānjyā hwèiyìde (yǒu)... those who attended the conference (were)...

tsānjyā hwèiyìde forms a clause, perhaps with rén left out at the end. cf. Selection 1, Voc.B-8

9. 莫洛托夫 Mwòlwòtwōfū N: Molotov

10. 艾登 Aìdēng N: Eden

11. 皮杜爾 Pídùěr N: Bidault

12. 杜勒斯 Dùlèisz̄ N: Dulles

13 朝鮮 Cháusyan N: Korea (Cháusyan, now used by North Korea, is a transliterated name from Chosan)

14. 外務相 wàiwùsyàng N: Foreign Minister

15. 南日 Nánr̀ N: Nam Il

16. 大韓民國	Dàhán Míngwó	N: Republic of Korea (the name used by South Korea)
韓國	Hángwó	N: Korean Republic
民國	míngwó	N: a republic
17. 澳大利亞	Aùdàlìyǎ	N: Australia
18. 比利時	Bǐlìshŕ	N: Belgium
19. 加拿大	Jyānádà	N: Canada
20. 哥倫比亞	Gēlwúnbǐyǎ	N: Colombia
21. 阿比西尼亞	Ābǐsyīníyǎ	N: Ethiopia (or Abyssinia)
22. 希臘	Syīlà	N: Greece
23. 盧森堡	Lúsēnbǎu	N: Luxembourg
24. 荷蘭	Hélán	N: the Netherlands (Holland)
25. 新西蘭	Syīnsyīlán	N: New Zealand
26. 菲律賓	Fēilyùbīn	N: the Philippines
27. 泰國	Tàigwó	N: Thailand
28. 土耳其	Tǔěrchí	N: Turkey
29. 通過	tūnggwò	V/CV: pass (resolutions) through
30. 由……担任……主席	yóu...dānrèn...jǔsyí	CV-V-O: Cf. Selection 3, Voc. B-22
31. 那拉底親王	Nàlādì Chīnwáng	N: Prince Wan Waithayakon

32. 為(了)	wèi(le)	CV:	for the purpose of...
33. 討論	taǔlwùn	V/N:	discuss/discussion
34. 對…來說	dwèi... láishwō	Ph:	as far as...is concerned, on the part of...
35. 瑞士	Rwèishr̀	N:	Switzerland
36. (會)議程(序)	(hwèi)yi-chéng(syù)	N:	agenda (of a meeting)
37. 休會	syōuhwèi	VO:	adjourn a meeting
38. 將	jyāng	A:	a word indicating the future (literary)

<u>Jyāng</u>, as an adverb, has to be used before either a verb or a coverb, as in the above case.

It is to be remembered that <u>jyāng</u>, when used as a coverb interchangeable with the colloq. <u>bǎ</u>, invariably precedes a noun.

39. 於	yú	CV:	at, in, to, than (literary)

It is a dative word implying the meaning of "with respect to", very frequently used in literary Chinese.

(1) It means "on", "in", or "at" when used before a TW or PW, corresponding to the colloquial dzài. E.g.

死於上海 sž yú Shànghǎi
died in Shanghai

於昨日離此 yú dzwór lí tsž
left here yesterday

(2) Implying "with respect to", <u>yú</u> may be

interpreted to mean "to", "from", "than", etc. E.g.

二百年於今 èrbainyán yú jīn
200 years from or up to now

A求助於B A chyóu jù yú B.
A seeks help from B.

(3) It may be used for comparison purposes, E.g.

A大於B A dà yú B.
A is bigger than (with respect to) B.

苛政猛於虎 Kējèng měng yú hǔ.
Tyranny is fiercer than a tiger.

(4) It indicates the passive voice introducing the agent of action. E.g.

A敗於B A bài yú B.
A was defeated by (with respect to) B.

(5) Yú goes sometimes with a TW or a PW, forming a phrase.

於....中 same as dzài...jūng

於....之上 same as dzài...shàng

於....(以)前 same as dzài...(yi)chyán

Common compounds with yú include:

dwèiyu 對於 CV: with respect to

gwānyu 關於 CV: regarding, concerning

jr̀yu 至於	CV: as for
yóuyu 由於	CV: owing to, due to
yúshr̀ 於是	MA: thereupon, then
(yǒu)jyànyu (有)鑒於	CV: in view of

NOTES

This Selection gives the student ample opportunity to tackle foreign names transliterated into Chinese. Close attention should be paid to the names of important foreign places as well as persons, many of which have an established Chinese rendering.

Constant reviewing of the rules regulating transliteration, as given in the Appendix, will be of benefit to the student.

EXERCISES

I. Translate into Chinese:

1. 此人 2. 此事 3. 此後 4. 致謝
5. 有關問題 6. 有關的事項
7. 逐字研究

II. Translate into English the following phrases or clauses with yú:

1. 於開會時
2. 於離此之後
3. 於啓程前
4. 於去年十二月五日起
5. 將於兩週之内開幕
6. 中國敗於日本。

III. Translate:

1. 你在這裏担任甚麽工作？
2. 據美國政府宣佈，美國總統明日將召開一個重要會議，討論關於東南亞洲的各項問題。
3. 昨天是法國國慶日，我國總統昨天上午代表我國政府及人民向法國致一賀電。
4. 會議的議程已於昨天順利通過。
5. 下次會議訂於明日上午九時舉行。

SELECTION VI

1. 據新華社日內瓦電:外交部部長會議已於四月二十六日下午二時在此間開幕.參加會議者有中國外交部部長,蘇聯外交部部長,美國國務卿等人.

2. 據稱,會議主席由泰國,蘇聯,英國三國首席代表輪流擔任.

3. 泰國首席代表担任第一天大會主席.他致辭說,這次召開外交部部長會議是為了討論亞洲各項問題.對中國來說,這個會議很重要.

4. 這次會議是在瑞士日內瓦舉行的,所以,瑞士政府向大會致一賀電.

5. 主席於宣佈議程後,大會宣告休會.下次會議主席將由蘇聯首席代表担任.

6. 國際聯盟是第一次世界大戰以後組成的.現在,雖然已經沒有這個組織,可是,日內瓦湖邊上有一個高樓,叫國聯大廈.

SELECTION 7

Fifth Anniversary of the Sino-Soviet Alliance Observed

慶祝中蘇同盟條約簽訂第五周年
中國駐蘇大使舉行招待會
布爾加寧莫洛托夫等出席

紐約時報十五日載莫斯科電：中華人民共和國駐蘇聯大使劉曉，十四日在莫斯科舉行盛大招待會，慶祝中蘇友好同盟互助條約簽訂第五周年。

應邀出席招待會的，有蘇聯政府的重要領導人物，其中包括蘇聯部長會議主席布爾加寧、蘇聯部長會議副主席兼外交部長莫洛托夫、蘇聯部長會議副主席兼電力站部長馬林科夫等。在應邀出席的各國駐蘇大使中，有英國駐蘇大使海特。

在招待會上，劉曉大使首先致詞說，正當美國帝國主義者在遠東製造緊張局勢的時候，中蘇兩國締結的友好同盟互助條約具有特別重要的意義。他對蘇聯在亞洲和歐洲執行的外交政策表示支持，並對蘇聯給予中國的援助表示感謝。

蘇聯部長會議主席布爾加寧致詞，指出中蘇友好同盟互助條約的主要作用是維護和平。他並表示：中國不但獲得蘇聯的同情，而且，在需要的時候，更可以由蘇聯獲得援助。

（紐約華僑日報一九五五年二月十六日）

Vocabulary A - New Characters

1. 盟		méng	BF: an alliance/to swear
	同盟	túngméng	N: alliance
	盟國	ménggwó	N: allied states
2. 簽		chyān	V: sign
	簽字	chyān dž	VO: sign name
	簽名	chyān míng	VO: sign name
3. 訂		dìng	V: settle, fix
	簽訂	chyāndìng	V: sign, conclude (treaty, contract, etc.)
4. 領		lǐng	V: lead
	首領	shǒulǐng	N: leader
5. 導		dǎu	V: lead, guide
	領導	lǐngdǎu	V/N: lead/guidance, leadership
6. 詞		tsź	N: word, phrase
	致詞	jr̀ tsź	VO: give a public speech (interchangeable with 致辭)
7. 帝		dì	N: emperor
	帝國	dìgwó	N: empire
	帝國主義	dìgwójǔyì	N: imperialism

	Character	Romanization		Definition
	帝國主義者	dìgwójǔyìjě	N:	an imperialist country
8.	製	jr̀	V:	make, manufacture
	製造	jr̀dzàu	V:	manufacture, create
9.	締	dì	BF:	closely joined, a connection
	締結	dìjyé	V:	make or conclude (a treaty), form (an alliance)
10.	示	shr̀	V:	manifest, illustrate; order
	表示	byǎushr̀	V:	express
	指示	jř̌shr̀	V/N:	order, instruct/instructions
11.	歐	Ōu	PW:	Europe
	歐洲	Ōujōu	PW:	Europe
12.	執	jŕ	V:	hold, manage
	執行	jŕsyíng	V:	enforce, carry out, exercise (power, etc.)
13.	策	tsè	BF:	scheme, policy
	政策	jèngtsè	N:	policy
14.	維	wéi	V:	maintain
	維護	wéihù	V:	safeguard
	維持	wéichŕ	V:	maintain, keep
15.	予	yú	V:	give (lit.)

給予	gěiyú	V:	give (a synonym compound)
16. 援	ywán	BF:	help, assist
援助	ywánjù	V/N:	aid, help
17. 需	syū	V:	need
需要	syūyàu	V/N:	need

Vocabulary B - New Expressions and Structural Analysis

1. 條約	tyáuywē	N:	a treaty
公約	gūngywē	N:	a multilateral treaty
2. 駐蘇大使	jù Sū dàshř		cf. Selection 3, Voc. B-9
3. 招待會	jāudàihwèi	N:	a reception (party)
招待	jāudài	V:	to entertain (in the sense of "to receive")
4. 劉曉	Lyóu Syǎu	N:	Liu Hsiao
5. 友好	yǒuhǎu	N:	friendship, goodwill
6. 互助	hùjù	N:	mutual help
7. 應邀出席.....的	yìng ywē chūsyí ...de		those who attended... cf. Selection 6, Voc. B-7

A literary rendering of the above will be yìng ywē chūsyí...jě. 者.

8. 人物 rénwù N: personage, a man of standing

9. 部長會議 Bùjǎnghwèiyì N: Council of Ministers (Soviet Union)

10. 外交部長 wàijyāubùjǎng This is a contraction of wàijyāubù bùjǎng

11. 電力站部 Dyànlìjànbù N: Ministry of Power Stations

12. 馬林科夫 Mǎlínkēfū N: Malenkov

13. 海特 Hǎitè N: Hayter

14. 在⋯上 dzài...shàng Ph: on..., at...

A placeword or a scene is usually inserted between dzài and shàng.

在陸地上	dzài lùdìshang	on land
在飛機場上	dzài fēijīchǎngshang	in the airfield
在會議上	dzài hwèiyìshang	at the conference

In addition to the above dzài...shàng may take expressions of an abstract nature, having the meaning of 'in respect of' or 'in the field of'. E.g.

在⋯基礎上	dzài...jīchǔshang	on the basis (or foundation) of...
在政治上	dzài jèngjrshang	in politics, politically
在文字改革上	dzài wéndz gǎigéshang	on the reform of the written language

There is a phrase similar in structure as, but opposite in meaning to, the above one:

在····下 dzài...syà under...

在···領導下 dzài...lǐngdǎusyà under the leadership of

15. 首先 shǒusyān A: at first, first of all (a synonym compound)

16. 正當····的時候 jèngdāng...de shŕhou Ph: when (or while)...

17. 遠東 Ywǎndūng PW: the Far East

18. 緊張 jǐnjāng SV: tense

19. 局勢 jyúshr̀ N: situation, circumstances

20. 具有·····意義 jyùyǒu...yìyì VO: be of...significance

具有 jyùyǒu V: have, possess (a synonym compound)

意義 yìyì N: significance

21. 對·····表示 dwèi...byǎushr̀... CV-V: to express... concerning...

The pattern is:

對(對於) (N)...V V...at (in, with,etc.)N

22. 指出	jř̌chū	V: point out
23. 作用	dzwòyùng	N: function, purpose, effect
24. 不但…而且…	búdàn... érchyě...	Ph: not only...but also...
不僅…而且…	bùjǐn...érchyě	Ph: not only.. but... (jǐn, only)
而且	érchyě	A: moreover, furthermore
25. 同情	túngchíng	N: sympathy
26. 由	yóu	CV: from

Yóu usually precedes a personal PN, a PW or a TW; it is interchangeable with dż 自 or the colloquial tsúng 從 . cf. Selection 3, Voc. B-22

EXERCISES

I. Translate into English:

1. 在軍事上
2. 在海面上
3. 在經濟發展上
4. 在中國歷史上
5. 在招待會上
6. 在王市長主持下
7. 在中美兩國合作下

II. Translate into English:

1. 西歐很多國家需要美國的援助.
2. 我們對政府的各項政策,應當支持.
3. 中蘇締結的同盟條約,兩國外交部長將於明天上午簽字.
4. 此事意義很大.

III.

1. 中華人民共和國和蘇聯締結之友好同盟互助條約是一九五〇年二月十四日在莫斯科簽訂的。其時,斯大林(Szdàlín, STALIN)還活着。毛澤東到蘇聯去訪問。這個條約就是毛澤東此次訪問的結果。

2. 中蘇同盟條約的主要作用,據稱,為維護遠東和平。這個條約不僅對於遠東局勢,而且對於世界和平,都具有很大的意義。

3. 據紐約時報所載莫斯科消息,我國駐蘇大使館於一九五五年二月十四日舉行招待會,慶祝中蘇締結同盟的第五周年。

4. 我國駐蘇大使首先致詞,說明此次舉行招待會之意義。然後,他指出美國帝國主義者正在遠東製造緊張局勢。

55. 我國駐蘇大使又稱,他對於蘇聯的亞洲和歐洲政策,一定支持。最後,他對蘇聯給予我國的援助和同情,表示感謝。

SELECTION 8

Standing Committee of National People's Congress Meets; Kwangtung's Governor Makes Report

全國人民代表大會常委會會議
陶鑄報告粵省僑務工作
毛主席任命張霖之為
第三機械工業部
長

（香港航訊）北京消息：全國人民
代表大會常務委員會在四月八日、
九日先後舉行了第十、第十一次會
議。

在第十次會議上，聽取了四川

省省長李大章關於四川省農業生產和農村工作的報告。

在第十一次會議上，聽取了廣東省省長陶鑄關於廣東省農業生產和華僑問題的工作報告。這次會議還根據國務院提出的議案，通過決定設立中華人民共和國第三機械工業部，負責領導地方國營、公私合營之合作社和私營的機械、電機工業；批准國務院設立城市建設總局；通過了任命事項。

又訊：中華人民共和國主席毛澤東九日根

據全國人民代表大會常務委員會第十一次會議通過的決定，任命張霖之爲中華人民共和國第三機械工業部部長。

(華僑日報一九五五年四月十九日)

Vocabulary A - New Characters

1. 粵	Ywè	PW: abbr. for Kwangtung Province
2. 械	syè	BF: implements, mechanical contrivance
機械	jīsyè	N: mechanism, machinery
軍械	jyūnsyè	N: weapons of war
3. 航	háng	BF: to sail/navigation (sea or air)
航空	hángkūng	N: aviation
航海	hánghǎi	V/N: navigate/navigation
4. 案	àn	N: a law-case, a proposal
議案	yìàn	N: a proposal (on agenda)
5. 負	fù	V: to bear on back
6. 責	dzé	N: responsibility
責任	dzérèn	N: responsibility
負責	fùdzé	SV/VO: be responsible for, take the responsibility of
7. 營	yíng	V: to manage (trade, etc.)
經營	jīngyíng	V: manage
8. 批	pī	V/N: to comment upon, endorse a petition, a batch
9. 准	jwǔn	V: approve

批准	pījwǔn	V/N: ratify, approve/ ratification, approval

Vocabulary B - New Expressions and Structural Analysis

1. 常委會	Chángwěihwèi	N: abbr. of Chángwù 常務 Wěiywánhwèi 委員會
2. 陶鑄	Táu Jù	N: Tao Chu, name of the present Governor of Kwangtung Province
3. 僑務	chyáuwù	N: affairs of citizens overseas (or residing in foreign countries)

Wù here stands for shrwù 事務. Similar expressions include:

國務	gwówù	N: national affairs
校務	syàuwù	N: school affairs

4. 任命	rènmìng	V/N: appoint/appointment
現任	syànrèn	the present
前(任)	chyán(rèn)	the former
新任	syīnrèn	newly appointed

These expressions precede the name of office. For instance,

前(任)市長 chyán(rèn) shrjǎng
the former Mayor

升任	shēngrèn...	V: be promoted to...

調任	dyàurèn	V:	be transferred (from one post to)
5. 張霖之	Jāng Línjr̄	N:	Chang Lin-chih
6. 第三機械工業部	Dìsān Jīsyè Gūngyè Bù	N:	the Third Ministry of Machine Building
工業	gūngyè	N:	industry
7. 先後	syānhòu	MA:	successively
8. 聽取	tīngchyǔ	V:	to hear, listen to
9. 省長	shěngjǎng	N:	governor of a province
10. 李大章	Lǐ Dà-jāng	N:	Lì Ta-chang
11. 廣東省	Gwǎngdūng Shěng	PW:	Kwangtung Province
12. 根據	gēnjyù	CV:	according to; in compliance with
13. 提出	tíchū	V:	put forward, submit
14. 設立	shèlì	V/N:	set up/establishment
15. 地方	dìfāng	N/SV:	place/local
16. 公私合營	gūng sz̄ héyíng		managed jointly by public and private (funds)

Gūng and sz̄, two antonyms, are placed in juxtaposition requiring no "and" to link them. Similar expressions include:

東南西北	dūng nán syī běi	N:	east, south, west, north
中美英	Jūng Měi Yīng	N:	China, U.S., U.K. (cf. headline of Selection 8)

17. 合作社	hédzwòshè	N:	cooperative stores
合作	hédzwò	V/N:	cooperate/cooperation
18. 電機	dyànjī	BF:	electrical
19. 城市建設總局	Chéngshr̀ Jyànshè Dzǔng Jyú	N:	General Board of Urban Redevelopment
20. 總	dzǔng	BF:	general
總局	dzǔngjyú	N:	general office
總司令	dzǔngszlīng	N:	commander-in-chief

NOTES

1. Names of China's provinces consist almost exclusively of two characters. These may be abbreviated to one character, which is a common practice for use in telegrams for the sake of economy, and the same practice is sometimes followed in newspapers as many news stories are transmitted telegraphically.

   Some of the abbreviated names retain one of the original characters and usually the more important one.

浙江	Chekiang (Jèjyāng)	浙	(Jè)
江蘇	Kiangsu (Jyāngsū)	蘇	(Sū)
陝西	Shensi (Shǎnsyī)	陝	(Shǎn)
四川	Szechwan (Sz̀chwān)	川	(Chwān)
台灣	Taiwan (Táiwān)	台	(Tái)

Other provincial names in abbreviated form may use a character entirely different from those in the original, for historical or other reasons. E.g.

福建 Fukien (Fújyàn) 閩 (Mǐn)

湖南 Hunan (Húnán) 湘 (Syāng)

湖北 Hupei (Húběi) 鄂 (È)

廣東 Kwangtung (Gwǎngdūng) 粵 (Ywè)

雲南 Yunnan (Yúnnán) 滇 (Dyān)

Some important cities in China also have their names abbreviated:

上海 Shanghai (Shànghǎi) 滬 (Hù)

天津 Tientsin (Tyānjing) 津 (Jīn)

重慶 Chungking (Chúngchìng) 渝 (Yú)

成都 Chengtu (Chéngdū) 蓉 (Rúng)

廣州 Canton (Gwǎngjōu) 穗 (Swèi)

The above is by no means a complete list of provinces in China.

EXERCISES

I. Translate into English:

1. 醫院院務會議
2. 前紐約市長
3. 新任美國駐法大使
4. 升任部長
5. 郵政總局
6. 大批貨物
7. 分批前往

II. Translate into English:

1. 昨天開會時通過很多議案.
2. 我們都在王總統領導下工作.
3. 那個東西是國營的,是私人經營的?
4. 新任法國駐華大使昨天到達上海.

1. 在中國大陸上,政府一切政策必須由全國人民代表大會常務委員會通過。政府之重要任命事項,必須經過全國人民代表大會常務委員會批准。

2. 全國人民代表大會常常聽取政府各負責人之工作報告。

3. 據香港消息,在全國人民代表大會常務委員會第十次會議上,四川省省長作了關於四川省農業生產和農村工作的報告。

4. 在第十一次會議上,廣東省省長報告廣東省農業生產及華僑問題。

5. 此外,全國人民代表大會常委會在其第十一次會議上決定設立第三機械工業部,並通過任命張霖之為部長。

6. 據政府宣佈,新設立之第三機械工業部之主要責任為領導:(一)國營和公私合營之合作社,(二)私營之機械工業及電機工業。

SELECTION 9

Soviet Union Blames U.S. and U.K.
for Forming Military Bloc in Near East

美英在中東組織軍事集團
蘇外交部就此發表聲明
指出美英此舉威脅蘇聯安全

合衆社莫斯科十七日電：蘇聯外交部十六日就西方國家在中、近東組織軍事集團問題發表聲明，指出西方國家這一行動嚴重地威脅蘇聯的安全。

蘇聯外交部的聲明指控以美國

為首的西方集團企圖把中、近東變為戰場，和把中、近東人民淪為殖民地奴隸。

聲明說，除非西方國家的政策改變，否則蘇聯政府將向聯合國提出控訴。

紐約十八日訊：合眾社記者自華盛頓報道，美國官方人物正根據杜勒斯國務卿的指示，擬定「廣泛的中東計劃」。這個「計劃」的目的，是為了使美國進一步滲入中東地區。

（華僑日報一九五五年四月十九日）

Vocabulary A - New Characters

1. 集	jí	V:	assemble
集團	jítwán	N:	bloc
2. 威	wēi	BF:	pomp, power
3. 嚴	yán	SV:	stern, strict
嚴重	yánjùng	SV/A:	serious/gravely
4. 控	kùng	V:	accuse, charge
指控	jřkùng	V/N:	accuse, denounce/ charge
控訴	kùngsù	V/N:	accuse/charge, a law suit
5. 企	chǐ	BF:	to look for, stand expectant
企圖	chǐtú	V:	attempt
6. 淪	lwún	V:	be lost, degrade into
7. 殖	jŕ (chŕ)	V:	plant, colonize
殖民地	jŕmíndì	N:	a colony
8. 奴	nú	N:	slave
9. 否	fǒu	P/A:	not, no (literary)
是否	shr̀fǒu	AV:	is it or is it not, whether or not
否認	fǒurèn	V:	deny
10. 則	dzé	A:	then (as in "if... then"), same as the colloq. jyòu/yet, on the other hand

否則	fǒudzé	A: otherwise (literary), same as the colloq. <u>yàuburán</u>.
11. 擬	nǐ	V: draft (a plan, etc.) intend
擬定	nǐdìng	V: draft
12. 劃	hwà	BF: plan
計劃	jìhwà	V/N: plan

<u>Vocabulary B</u> - <u>New Expressions and Structural Analysis</u>

1. 中東	Jūngdūng	PW: Middle East
2. 近東	Jìndūng	PW: Near East
3. 軍事	jyūnshr̀	SV: military
4. 就	jyòu...	CV: with respect to, on

The pattern is <u>jyòu</u> N, V... . E.g.

就此V	jyòu tsž V...	with respect to this, V...
就…問題V	jyòu...wèntí,V...	with respect to the problem..., V...

5. 發表	fābyǎu	V: make public, proclaim
6. 聲明	shēngmíng	N/V: announcement/announce
7. 舉動	jyǔdùng	N: act
8. 威脅	wēisyè	V/N: to threaten/menace
9. 安全	ānchywán	SV/N: secure/safety,security

10. 行動 syíngdùng N: action, deed

11. ……地 ...de A: an adverbial ending

The following distinction is sometimes made:

的	attributive de	
底	possessive de, E.g.	wǒde shū 我底書
地	adverbial de	

12. 以美國為首的 yǐ Měigwo wéi shǒude ...headed by the U.S. (cf. Selection 1-B 8)

13. 把……V bǎ...V

Bǎ is a CV used to bring the object to the front of the main and invariably transitive verb. This transposition of words makes the object definite in nature and consequently more stressed.

14. 戰場 jànchǎng N: battlefield

15. 奴隸 núlì N: slave

16. 除非……否則…… chúfēi... fǒudzé... unless...otherwise...

17. 聯合國 Lyánhégwó N: United Nations

18. 報道(報導) bàudàu (bàudǎu) V/N: report

19. 官方 gwānfāng N: official circles (fāng for fāngmyàn)

20. 廣泛 gwǎngfàn SV: broad (in nature)

21. 目的 mùdì N: purpose

22. 使……V shř...V CV...V to make (or cause) ...V...

Shř is interchangeable with the colloq. ràng in the present case. This is again a case of verbal expressions in series since it is always followed by the main verb.

23. 進一步 jìn yíbù A: further
VO: go one step further

24. 滲入 shènrù V: infiltrate

25. 地區 dìchyū N: area, district

EXERCISES

I. Make sentences with:

1. 不僅····,而且····
2. 就(CV)····
3. 除非····,否則····
4. 使····

II. Translate into English:

1. 外交部王部長昨天就中日兩國簽訂同盟條約的問題,招待記者談話.
2. 官方消息:國防部張部長昨天晚上在其講演中,指出印度總理之訪問中國,使中印之友好關係更進一步.
3. 此事現在應當解決,否則,遠東和平就受威脅.

SELECTION IX

1. 聯合國於一九四五年成立 (CHÉNGLÌ, ESTABLISH) 其目的為維護世界和平。成立之時，只有五十一國。一九八六年春天，已達一百六十國之多。

2. 現在世界上共有一百九十個獨立 (DÚLÌ, INDEPENDENT) 的國家。其中五分之二是最近五十年才獨立的，第二次世界大戰之前還是殖民地。

3. 一個國家如果覺得自己的安全受到威脅，或是世界和平受到威脅，可以向聯合國提出，請聯合國解決。

4. 據莫斯科官方消息：西方國家在中東組織軍事集團。蘇聯政府就此發表一項聲明。蘇聯指控英美此舉之目的是企圖滲入中東地區，把中東變成戰場，把中東人民淪為英美之奴隸。

5. 蘇聯聲明並稱，此事非常嚴重，蘇聯之安全已經嚴重地受到威脅。西方國家應改變其中東政策，否則，蘇聯將在聯合國中提出控訴。

6. 聯合國安全理事會 (SECURITY COUNCIL) 共有十五個國家。據稱,主席由各國首席代表輪流担任,每次負責一個月。

7. 據美聯社駐聯合國記者報導,聯合國大會 (GENERAL ASSEMBLY) 昨日下午就非洲問題熱烈討論兩小時,今日上午又作進一步之討論,結果,擬定一項解决計劃。

8. 世界上現在有兩個大的集團。西方國家由美國領導。另外那個集團以蘇聯為首。有些國家,例如印度及幾個最近獨立的國家,不參加集團;它們的外交政策是中立 (jūnglì, NEUTRAL, NEUTRALITY) 的。

SELECTION 10

Earthquakes Reported in Western Yunnan and Tokyo

北平電台廣播

滇西地震嚴重

（四日合眾社東京電）據北平電台廣播，雲南省西部曾於去年十二月廿一日發生大地震。三百人斃命，一千五百卅七人受傷，房屋四萬座被毀，十萬零二千人無家可歸。（舊金山世界日報一九五二年一月四日）

Earthquakes Reported in Western Yunnan and Tokyo

東京地區
強烈地震

（美聯社東京一日電）今晨二時八分左右，東京區發生強烈的地震，使許多東京居民於驚恐中自床上逃出。中央氣象台說，今晨的地震，在東京橫濱間以及本州中部的大部份地區。此次地震除驚擾睡眠外，並未發生任何其他的損害。

（台北中央日報一九五一年十月二日）

Vocabulary A - New Characters

1.震	jèn	V:	shock, shake
地震	dìjèn	N/S-V:	earthquake
2.曾(曾)	tséng	A:	a word indicating an action (occuring in the past)
3.廿	nyàn	NU:	twenty
4.斃	bì	V:	kill, die a violent death
斃命	bìmìng	V:	be killed, be dead
5.卅	sā (sà)	NU:	thirty
6.座	dzwò	N/M:	seat/ M for houses, city wall, etc.
7.毀	hwěi	V:	destroy, demolish
8.歸	gwēi	V:	return (literary)
9.區	chyū	N:	region, area
地區	dìchyū	N:	region, zone
10.晨	chén	TW:	morning, dawn
早晨	dzǎuchén	TW:	morning
11.居	jyū	V:	dwell, reside (literary)
居民	jyūmín	N:	inhabitants, resident population
12.床(牀)	chwáng	N:	bed
13.央	yāng	BF:	the middle

中央	jūngyāng	N/SV:	center/central
14. 擾	rǎu	V/N:	disturb, annoy
15. 眠	myán	V/N:	sleep (literary)
睡眠	shwèimyán	N:	sleep (a synonym compound)
16. 未	wèi	A:	not (past), not yet (literary)
17. 損	swǔn	V/N:	damage, injure
損失	swǔnshr̄	V/N:	to lose/loss
損害	swǔnhài	N:	damage

Vocabulary B - New Expressions and Structural Analysis

北平	Běipíng	**PW:**	**Peking**
1. 滇	Dyān	PW:	abbr. for Yunnan Province
滇西	Dyānsyī	PW:	western part of Yunnan Province (syī for syībù)

Similar Expressions:

華北	Hwáběi	PW:	North China
華南	Hwánán	PW:	South China

but, 南韓; 西德; 東非; 東南亞.

2. 東京	Dūngjīng	PW:	Tokyo (Japan)
3. 發生	fāshēng	V/N:	occur, take place, occurence

An indefinite subject often follows the verb. For instance, syà yǔ (gwā fēngle, etc.) in which yǔ is used in the indefinite sense of 'rain'. However, in yǔ tíngle, yǔ becomes definite in nature - 'the rain' - and is used before the verb.

In the present case, fāshēng is an intransitive verb, and dàdìjèn the subject, indefinite in nature. Try to distinguish the following:

昨天發生大地震 Dzwótyan fāshēng dàdìjèn. (An earthquake occurred yesterday.)

地震發生以後.... dàdìjèn fāshēng yǐhòu,... (after the earthquake occurred, ...)

Further cases include:

来客(人)了;客(人)来了。

發生水災;水災發生以後.....

4. 房屋四萬座 fángwū sżwàn dzwò

The normal word order is NU-M-N. In literary Chinese the word order usually is N-NU-M, as here. Sometimes, M is even left out.

5. 被 bèi CV: a word indicating passive voice

6 無家可歸 wú jyā kě gwēi, to have no home to return to, homeless

The pattern is wú N kě V. Other phrases on the same pattern are:

無事可作 wú shr̀ kě dzwò, to have nothing to do

無法可治 wú fǎ kě jr̀ incurable

無話可說 wú hwà kě shwō, to have nothing to say

無地可容 <u>wú</u> <u>dì</u> <u>kě</u> <u>rúng</u>, without a leg to stand on

7. 強烈 chyánglyè SV: violent

8. 今晨 jīn chén TW: this morning

This semi-literary expression is an abbreviation of <u>jīntyān</u> <u>dzǎuchén</u> 今天早晨

Similary, <u>wǎn</u> stands for <u>wǎnshang</u>; <u>yè</u>, for <u>yèli</u>, and so on. Thus:

昨晚 dzwó wǎn TW: last evening or night

昨夜十時 dzwó yè shŕshŕ TW: 10 o'clock last night

明晨 míng chén TW: tomorrow morning

9. ....左右 ...dzwǒyòu N: in the neighborhood of, approximately (used as a suffix)

10. 許多 syǔdwō NU: many, a great many

11. 驚恐 jīngkǔng N: consternation, panic

12. 於...中 yú...jūng Ph: in the midst of..., cf. Selection 6, Voc. B-39 (5)

13. 氣象台 chìsyàngtái N: observatory

氣象 chìsyàng N: climatic conditions

14. 在....間 dzài...jyān Ph: between, among

15. 橫濱 Héngbīn PW: Yokohama

16. 本州 Běnjōu PW: Honshu (the main island of Japan)

17. 除...外 chú...wài Ph: besides, apart from...

除⋯⋯以外 same

除⋯⋯之外 same

18. 並 bìng A: indeed

This is a stress word usually used in a negative statement.

19. 任何 rènhé N: any (literary), same as the colloq. shémma in a statement.

Note

1. The Central Daily 中央日報 is an official organ of the Kuomintang (the Nationalist Party).

EXERCISES

I. Translate into English:

1. 昨夜十時 2. 明晚九時半
3. 今晚或明晨 4. 七月五日夜

II. Make sentences with:

1. 曾 2. 未 3. 被 4. 於⋯⋯中
5. 除⋯⋯外

III. Translate into English:

1. 除此以外，我們未受任何別的損失.
2. 昨夜此間曾發生地震一次.
3. 房屋被毀者很多.居民受傷者二百五十人.
4. 張大年昨被任為中國駐法大使.
5. 他將於明晨飛往美國.

PART ONE:

1. 其他地區
2. 前任國防部部長
3. 並未受傷
4. 曾於上月批准
5. 將於廿一日起程歸國
6. 將向法院提出控訴
7. 由一委員會負責
8. 根據總統之指示
9. 正當全場鼓掌之時
10. 正當歐洲局勢緊張之時
11. 使我們無話可說
12. 淪為殖民地之地位
13. 企圖滲入中東地區
14. 華北各省未受擾亂
15. 官方還未宣佈

PART TWO:

1. 據稱,一九〇六年四月,舊金山曾發生一次地震,並有大火。居民五百人斃命。損失很大。

2. 日本常有地震。一九二三年九月一日之地震為日本歷史上最大之一次。東京的三分之一及橫濱之大部分被毀。

3. 一九五〇年八月十五日印度東北部曾發生一次強烈地震。損害非常嚴重。

4. 一九六〇年五月,智利(JRLÌ, CHILE)發生兩次大地震。據官方公佈,有五千七百人斃命。無家可歸者幾百萬人。

5. 一九五一年十月一日日本本州中部所發生的地震不太嚴重,除驚擾居民睡眠外,並無任何損害。

SELECTION 11

Sino-American Defense Pact Ratification Documents to be Exchanged Today; Dulles Visiting Taiwan

中美共同防禦條約
定今午互換批准書

杜勒斯今再度訪華
中美舉行重要會議

（中央社訊）中美共同防禦條約定三日正午十二時在臺北市堡壘廳互換批准書。按照條約規定，經互換批准書後，中美共同防禦條約即正式生效。互換儀式中國方面將由外交部長葉公超代表，美國方面將由杜勒斯國務卿代表，並將邀請中美有關人員觀禮。

中美雙方軍事人員在中美共同防禦條約生效後，將於三日下午起在臺北舉行三天聯席會議，討論與條約有關之各項軍事問題，以適應當前臺灣海峽情勢。

（本報訊）美國國務卿杜勒斯定今日上午十時四十五分自馬尼拉乘專機飛抵臺北，預定作六小時之訪問。此爲杜勒斯國務卿第二次訪問自由中國。杜勒斯留臺期間，將以大部份時間與蔣總統及我國首長舉行會談，檢討中美兩國間有關問題。杜勒斯國務卿並將於今日中午代表美國方面，主持中美共同防禦條約互換批准書典禮。

（台北中央日報中華民國四十四年三月三日）

Vocabulary A - New Characters

1.禦	yù	V:	to ward off, defend
防禦	fángyù	V/N:	defend/defence
2.照	jàu	CV:	according to
按照	ànjàu	CV:	according to, in accordance with
3.即(卽)	jì	A:	then immediately (interchangeable with the colloq. jyòu.) presently
		V:	be (is, are, was, etc.) that is, namely
即將	jìjyāng	A:	presently, very shortly
立即	lìjì	A:	at once, immediately
....在即	...dzàijì	Ph:	... draw close,...be at hand (time)
4.效	syàu	N/SV:	efficacious, effectiveness
效力	syàulì	N:	efficacy, effectiveness
生效	shēng syàu	VO:	to become effective, to come into force
有效	yǒusyàu	SV:	efficacious, effective
5.與	yú	CV:	and, with (literary), interchangeable with the colloq. gēn.
6.峽	syá	N:	a gorge, strait
海峽	hǎisyá	N:	strait, (sea)channel

7. 抵	dǐ	V: arrive at, reach (literary)
飛抵	fēi dǐ	V: arrive by air
抵達	dǐdá	V: arrive, reach (a synonym compound)
8. 撿	jyǎn	V: examine
撿討	jyǎntǎu	V: review and discuss
9. 儀	yí	BF: ceremony, rites
儀式	yíshr̀	N: ceremony

Vocabulary B - New Expressions and Structural Analysis

1. 共同	gùngtúng	SV: mutual, common
2. 定	dìng	V: be scheduled
定於	dìngyú	V: be scheduled

dìng(yú) introduces a Time Word.

3. 今	jīn	TW: abbr. for jīntyān
今午	jīn wǔ	TW: abbr. for jīntyān jūngwǔ (or jèngwǔ)
4. 批准書	pījwǔnshū	N: instrument of ratification
5. 再度	dzàidù	A: once again
一度	yídù	TW: at one time formerly
數度	shùdù	A: (for) several times
6. 華	hwá	N: abbr. for China

7. 三日 VS 三天		sān r̀ means either "on the third" or "three days", whereas sān tyān means "three days".
8. 臺北市	Táiběishr̀	PW: (city of) Taipeh (shr̀, metropolis)
9. 堡壘廳	bǎulěitīng	PW: Fortress Hall
10. 規定	gwēidìng	N/V: provisions (in a treaty), to stipulate
11. 經…後,即…	jīng...hòu ji...	After..., then... (jīng, after)
…後,即…		V...hòu, jì V After..., then immediately V
12. 葉公超	Yè Gūng-chāu	N: Yeh Kung-ch'ao
13. 人員	rénywán	N: personnel
14. 觀禮	gwān lǐ	VO: watch the ceremony (lǐ for dyǎnlǐ 典禮)
15. 雙方	shwāngfāng	N: both sides, both parties (fāng for fāngmyàn)
16. 在…後	dzài...hòu	Ph: after..., cf. Selection 4, Voc. B-14
17. 於…起	yú...chǐ	Ph: starting..., as of... cf. Selection 6, Voc. B-39 (5)
18. 聯席會議	lyánsyí hwèiyì	N: joint meeting or session

19. 適應 shŕyìng V: to cope with, adapt/adjustment

20. 以 V yǐ V CV-V: so as to, to

This extremely useful chain of verbal expressions serves to amplify and describe the purpose of the previously stated thought. It conforms to the pattern:

S...V..., yǐ V... (so as to V...)

That is to say that <u>yi-V</u> is always used after the main verb in a sentence.

以適應	yǐ shŕyìng	so as to cope with
以便	yǐbyàn	in order to (facilitate)
以示	yǐshr̀	in order to express
以期	yǐchī	so as to (expect)
以資	yǐdz̄	so as to (serve to)
以致(於)	yǐjr̀(yu)	so as to -- usually followed by an untoward consequence

21. 當前 dāngchyán TW: the present, current (same as <u>mùchyán</u>)

22. 情勢 chíngshr̀ N: situation, trend of affairs

23. The second paragraph of the present Selection may be analyzed in detail as follows:

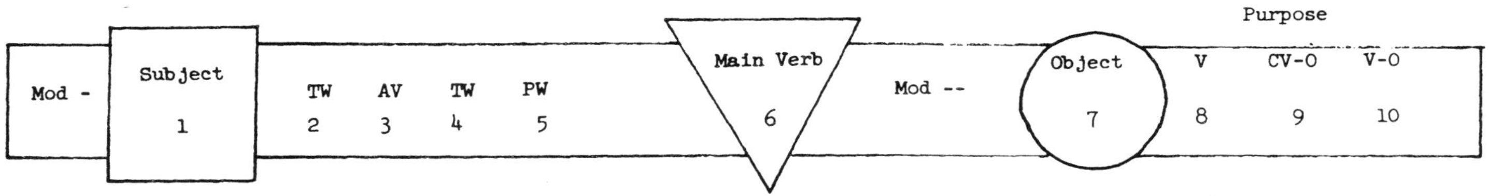

1. Jūng-Měi shwāngfān jyūnshr̀ RÉNYWÁN. (Rénywán is the subject, modified by all that precedes)

2. DZÀI Jūng-Měi gùngtúng fángyù tyáuywē shēngsyàu HÒU (Dzài introduces expression of relative time ending in (yǐ)hòu.

3. Jyāng is an AV indicating futurity.

4. YÚ sānr̀ syàwǔ CHǏ (Yú is equivalent to colloquial tsúng, a CV whose object is the TW sānr̀ syàwǔ. The clause ends in the V chǐ and gives the sense of starting from)

5. DZÀI Táiběi (Place expression)

6. JYǗSYÍNG (Main verb, predicate to the subject rénywán)

7. Sāntyān lyánsyí HWÈIYÌ (Hwèiyì is the object and is modified by the M sāntyān and lyánsyí)

8. TǍULWÙN (verb of purpose)

9. YÚ tyáuywē yǒugwānjr gèsyàng jyūnshr̀ WÈNTÍ (coverbial expression, yú being the CV and wèntí its object, the remaining words modify wèntí)

10. YǏ SHR̄YÌNG dāngchyán Táiwān Hǎisyá CHÍNGSHR̀ (This is a supplementary clause indicating the purpose of the doing mentioned above. Yǐ is a CV; shr̄yìng, a verb whose object is chíngshr̀.)

24. 本 běn BF: (one's) own, this

Běn is usually followed by a N, conveying the meaning of "this" or "the current".

本報	běn bàu	N: this newspaper
本月	běn ywè	TW: this month
本城	běn chéng	PW: this place/local
本人	běn rén	PN: one's self

25. 馬尼拉 Mǎnilā PW: Manila

26. 專機 jwānjī N: special airplane

27. 留⋯⋯期間 lyóu...chījyān Ph: during the stay at...

⋯⋯期間 ...chījyān TW: during the period of...

28. 以 N yǐ N

Yǐ primarily means "to take". With a N, as above, it forms as adverbial phrase and thus has to go before the main verb in a sentence, having the meaning of "with N" of the like. E.g.

以法文出版	yǐ Fàwén chūbǎn	be published in French
以武器援助日本	yǐ wǔchì ywánjǔ Rběn	to aid Japan with weapons
以⋯身份	yǐ...shēnfèn	in the capacity of...
以⋯名義	yǐ...míngyi	in the name of...

In addition to the above, yǐ N may be preceded by certain verbs. E.g.

給以大量軍援	gěi yǐ dàlyàng jyūnywán	to give military assistance in large quantities

yú díren yǐ dǎji
予敵人以打擊 to give the enemy a blow

* shī yǐ yālì to exert pressure
施以壓力

jyā yǐ dyàuchá
(對...)加以調查 (with respect to...) to investigate (lit. to impose onto it an investigation)

Furthermore, yǐ may assume the meaning of "because" or "because of" when followed by a N or a noun clause. E.g.

yǐ yǔ wèi lái did not come because of the rain
以雨未來

yǐ shr̀ máng wèi néng chyánwǎng
以事忙未能前往 didn't go because there was too much to be done

29. 首長 shǒujǎng N: chiefs, chief officials (cf. Selection 3, Voc. A- 9)

NOTES

1. From this Selection onward, no signs will be given for proper names. By now the student is fairly well equipped to work on them.

EXERCISE

I. Translate into English the following phrases with yǐ + V:

1. 以便進行
2. 以檢討遠東局勢
3. 以示慶賀
4. 以盡責任
5. 以免受害
6. 以致於此
7. 難以辦理
8. 藉以解決人口問題

II. Translate into English the following phrases or clauses with yǐ + N:

1. 以市長地位對全市市民演講
2. 以飛機五十架交與我國
3. 以五十票對三票通過
4. 以外交部長身份 (shēnfèn, capacity) 出席會議
5. 給以經濟援助
6. 予以抵抗
7. 告以當前局勢之緊張

III. Translate into English the following with yǐ + noun clause:

1. 以火車太慢，決乘飛機前往。
2. 日本總理以遠東局勢緊張，昨日飛往中國首都，與中國政府首長會談。

IV. Translate the present Selection into English.

PART ONE

1. 於明晨起
2. 留美期間
3. 定於本月廿一日啓程
4. 一度在我國工作
5. 再度宣佈
6. 法國政府首長
7. 儀式莊嚴
8. 於明日起有效
9. 現已無效
10. 經調查後
11. 飛抵台北之後
12. 將乘專機前往
13. 會談三日
14. 作五小時之會談
15. 即將抵華

PART TWO

1. 臺灣省包括台灣與澎湖列島(PÉNGHÚ LYÈDAU, Pescadores Islands)全省現有兩千萬人,其中漢人佔百分之九十以上.重要城市有台北,台中等.

2. 中國與美國於中華民國四十四年,即一九五五年,締結一項共同防禦條約,並於三月三日在台北市互換批准書.

3. 據台北中央日報所載消息,中美條約批准書互換儀式非常隆重.批准書交換之後,條約立即生效.

4. 按照條約規定,中美兩國軍事人員應不斷舉行聯席會議,檢討台灣海峽以及遠東之情勢.

5. 據中央社訊,美國國務卿曾到台北參加中美共同防禦條約批准書互換典禮.

6. 臺灣海峽不寬(kwān, WIDE)據稱,有的地方只有一百哩左右.

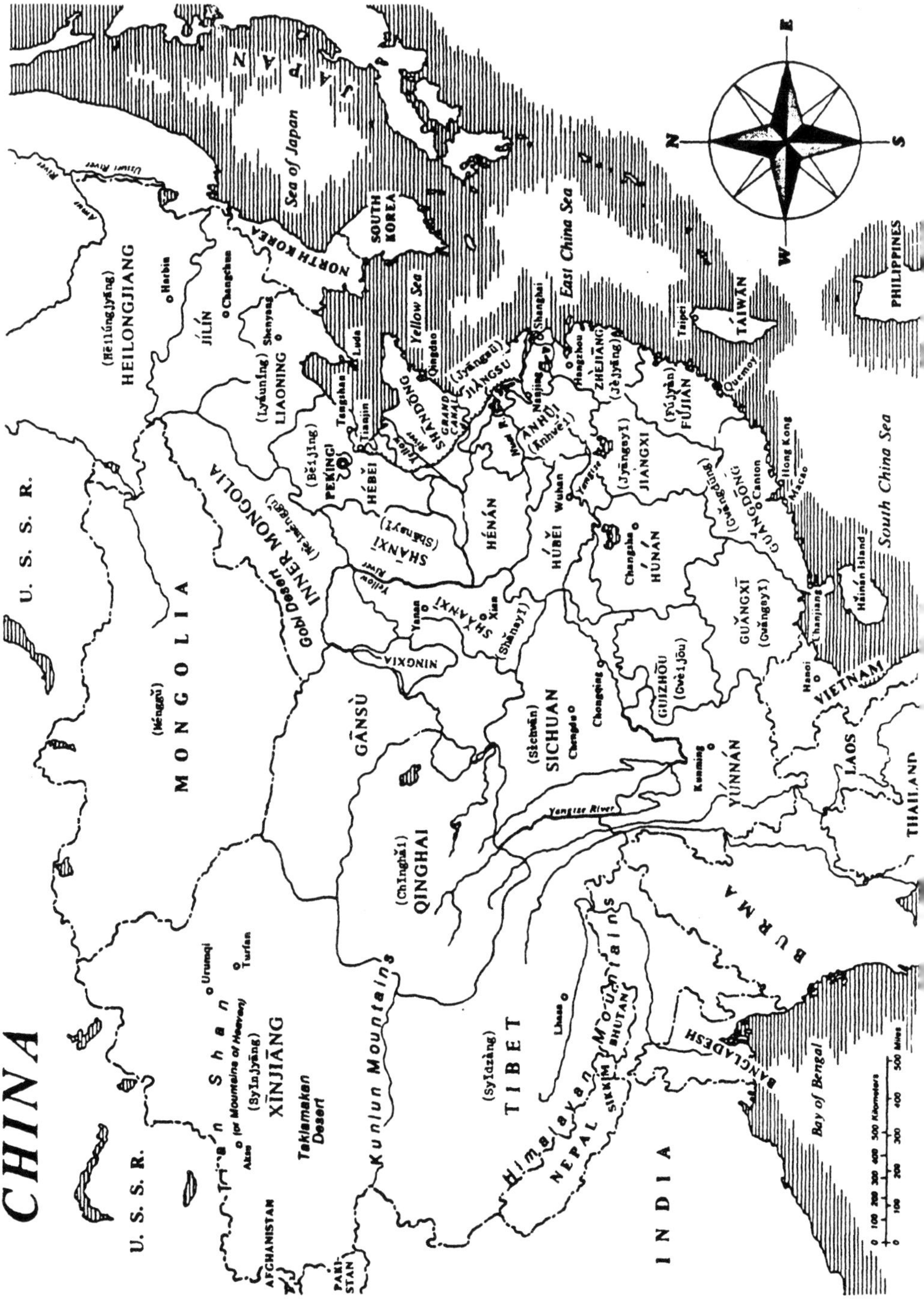

CHINA
U. S. S. R.
MONGOLIA
(Ménggǔ)
INNER MONGOLIA
Gobi Desert
HEILONGJIANG
(Hēilúngjyāng)
Harbin
JÍLÍN
Changchun
LIAONING
(Lyáuníng)
Shenyang
Luda
NORTH KOREA
SOUTH KOREA
Sea of Japan
JAPAN
Yellow Sea
East China Sea
South China Sea
PEKING
(Běijīng)
Tianjin
Tangshan
HÉBEI
SHANDŌNG
Qingdao
GRAND CANAL
JIANGSU
(Jyāngsū)
Shanghai
Nanjing
Hangzhou
ZHEJIANG
(Jèjyāng)
ANHUI
(Ānhwēi)
FUJIAN
(Fújyàn)
TÁIWĀN
Taipei
Quemoy
PHILIPPINES
SHANXI
(Shānsyī)
SHAANXI
(Shǎnsyī)
Xian
Yanan
HÉNÁN
HÚBEI
Wuhan
JIANGXI
(Jyāngsyī)
HUNAN
Changsha
GUǍNGDŌNG
(Gwǎngdūng)
Canton
Hong Kong
Macao
GUǍNGXĪ
(Gwǎngsyī)
Hǎinán Island
Chanjiang
Hanoi
VIETNAM
LAOS
THAILAND
GUIZHOU
(Gwèijōu)
Chongqing
SICHUAN
(Szchwān)
Chengdu
YÚNNÁN
Kunming
Yangtze River
Yellow River
Ussuri River
Amur River
NINGXIA
GĀNSÙ
QINGHAI
(Chīnghǎi)
TIBET
(Syīdzàng)
Lhasa
XĪNJIĀNG
(Syīnjyāng)
Urumqi
Turfan
Aksu
Tian Shan (or Mountains of Heaven)
Taklamakan Desert
Kunlun Mountains
Himalayan Mountains
NEPAL
SIKKIM
BHUTAN
BURMA
BANGLADESH
INDIA
Bay of Bengal
AFGHANISTAN
PAKISTAN
N
S
E
W

SELECTION 12

Sino-American Defense Pact Ratification Documents to be Exchanged Today; Dulles Visiting Taiwan (cont'd.)

杜勒斯今再度訪華
中美舉行重要會議
討論實施中美條約事宜

（本報訊）據官方發表，美國務卿杜勒斯今日訪問我國之日程，業經中美雙方排定如次：上午十時四十五分抵達臺北機場，下機後即赴美國大使館休息，十一時在美大使館與美國方面人員舉行會議，十二時參加中美共同防禦條約互換批准書典禮，十二時三十分在總統官邸覲謁　蔣總統，並應　蔣總統夫婦午宴，下午四時十五分在美國大使館舉行記者招待會，四時四十五分赴機場，五時離臺返美。

據悉：杜勒斯國務卿於參加中美共同防禦條約批准書換文儀式後，即將就中美共同防禦條約有關問題在總統官邸與　蔣總統及中美雙方高級官員有所商談。關整個臺灣海峽之防務部署，亦將屬於商談內容之一。

（中央社馬尼拉二日專電）刻在此間訪問的美國務卿杜勒斯預定明晨七時三十分飛往臺北，作五小時的訪問，以與中華民國政府領袖會商實施中美共同防禦條約事宜。

此間美國大使館於今日正午就杜勒斯赴臺訪問事發表聲明如次：「美國國務卿杜勒斯應中華民國之邀請，在其返美途中在臺北停留，以便參加中美共同防禦條約批准書的互換，這將使中美共同防禦條約付諸實施。」

（台北中央日報中華民國四十四年三月三日）

Vocabulary A - New Characters

1. 施	shr̄	BF:	carry out
實施	shŕshr̄	V/N:	carry out/implementation
施行	shr̄syíng	V:	carry out, put into practice
2. 邸	dǐ	N:	official residence
官邸	gwāndǐ	N:	official residence
3. 謁	yè	V:	to visit (superior)
4. 赴	fù	V:	go (literary)
5. 返	fǎn	V:	return (literary)
6. 悉	syì	V:	know, understand (literary)
據悉	jyù syì	CV-V:	it is known that
7. 亦	yì	A:	also (literary)
8. 袖	syòu	N:	sleeves
領袖	lǐngsyòu	N:	leader (cf. Selection 7, Voc. A- 4)
9. 途	tú	N:	way, road (literary), (cf. present Selection Voc. B 18)
10. 付	fù	V:	hand over, pay, entrust

Vocabulary B - New Expressions and Structural Analysis

1. 事宜 shìyí N: matters

2. 日程 rchéng N: program (or schedule for the day)

3. 業 yè A: already (literary)

業已 yèyǐ A: already

4. 經 jīng CV: through, after

Jīng primarily is a V, meaning "to go through" or "pass through". But when followed by a N ≠ V, as here, it does no longer assume the position of a full-fledged verb, and indeed it seems to become a co-verb with the function of introducing the agent of action in a passive voice.

業經中美雙方排定
yèjīng Jūng Měi shwāngfāng páidìng
(program) that has already been arranged by the Chinese and U. S. circles

5. 如次 rútsz̀ Ph: as follows (lit.)

Similar expressions include:

如下 rúsyà Ph: as follows

如後 rúhòu Ph: as follows

如上 rúshàng Ph: as above

6. 機 jī N: airplane (abbr. of fēijī)

機場 jīchǎng N: airfield

下機 syà jī VO: get off an airplane

專機	jwānjī	N: special airplane
搭機	dā jī	VO: board an airplane
7. 覲謁	jǐnyè	V: to pay a visit to (the chief of a state)
8. 記者招待會	jìjějāudàihwèi	N: press conference
9. 換文	hwàn wén	VO: exchange of documents
10. 所 V	swǒ-V	

Swǒ-V forms a nominal expression.
This form is frequently preceded in literary Chinese by the verb yǒu. E.g.

yǒu swǒ-shāngtán 有所商談	to have something to discuss, to have a discussion
yǒu swǒ-bàugàu 有所報告	to have something to report, to give a report
yǒu swǒ-jǐshr̀ 有所指示	to have instructions to give, to give instructions
"gè yǒu swǒ-cháng" 各有所長	Each has his (its) good points.

11. 聞	wén	V: it is learned (or heard) that

When it is used to introduce a sentence, wén assumes the meaning of "it is learned that".

12. 部署	bùshǔ	N: deployment (military)
13. 內容	nèirúng	N: contents

14.⋯之一	....jr̄ yī	Ph: one of....
15.刻	kè	TW: at present
16.中華民國	Jūnghwámíngwó	N: Republic of China
17.就⋯事	jyòu...shr̀	with respect to the matter of (or that)...

Functioning adverbially, "jyòu...shr̀" precedes the V of the sentence. cf. Selection 9 Voc. B-4

18.在⋯途中	dzài...tújūng	Ph: on one's way to...
19.以便	yǐ byàn	Ph: so as to (cf. Selection 11, Voc.B-21 and examples)
20.諸	jū	PN: a fusion of <u>jr̄</u> <u>yú</u> 之於
	fù jū shŕshr̄ 付諸實施	Ph: put it into realization

In addition, <u>jū</u>, when used as a BF in front of a N, has the meaning of "various" or "many".

jū shr̀ 諸事	various matters

EXERCISES

SELECTION XII

PART ONE

1. 下機之前
2. 亦將前往
3. 以便實施
4. 據官方宣佈
5. 出席記者招待會
6. 謁見　總統
7. 赴華訪問
8. 發表聲明如下
9. 預定今晚返華
10. 以示慶賀
11. 內容業已宣佈
12. 業於今晨七時抵達
13. 日程還未排定
14. 軍事部署事宜
15. 對本年之農業生產有所報告

PART TWO

1. 中央日報為台灣最大的報紙之一。其所有社論代表我國政府立場。此外，聞台灣還有許多其他大報。

2. 據悉，第二次世界大戰之後，美國與許多國家締結同盟。一九四九年四月，美國與英法意大利西德等國簽訂北大西洋公約，共同担任大西洋之防務。

3. 北大西洋公約組織現有十五個國家。各國政府領袖常舉行會議，商討共同防禦事宜。

4. 在太平洋，美英法澳大利亞泰國等八國組織東南亞公約組織。此為一九五四年九月之事。此外，美國與日本於一九五一年曾簽共同防禦條約。美國與澳大利亞新西蘭亦訂有共同防禦條約。

5. 美洲各國設有美洲國家國組織，共同負責美洲地區之防務。參加此組織者，於一九四八年，共有二十一國。聞加拿大未參加。

SELECTION 13

Premier Yü Reports to the Legislative Yuan on Administration Programs

俞院長向立院報告

政府施政計劃綱要

與盟邦聯合行動對抗

共黨侵略

（本報訊）立法院昨日舉行第七次秘密會議，邀行政院長、主計長、財政部長報告中華民國四十四年度中央政府總預算案編製經過，並備質詢。

會議在中山堂舉行。由副院長

黃國書主席，行政院俞院長各政務委員暨各部會首長列席。首由行政院長俞鴻鈞就施政計劃提出報告，繼由主計長龐松舟、財政部長徐柏園，對總預算案編製經過，分別加以說明。

(本報訊)行政院長俞鴻鈞，昨天列席立法院第七次秘密院會，對四十四年度的施政計劃綱要及總預算編製情形，作詳盡的報告。俞院長在綱要中說：臺灣是我反攻復國的基地；收復國土，解救大陸同胞是我最神聖最基本的責任。俞院長指出：現階段反共抗俄的任務是：「我們的行動要與盟邦的行動相配合，俾以聯合行動，有效對抗國際共產集團的侵略。」

（台北中央日報中華民國四十四年四月十三日）

Vocabulary A - New Characters

1.綱	gāng	N: bond, principles
綱要	gāngyàu	N: a summary
大綱	dàgāng	N: an outline
2.抗	kàng	V: oppose, resist
對抗	dwèikàng	V: oppose, resist
抵抗	dǐkàng	V/N: resist/resistence
3.侵	chīn	V: invade (in bad sense), transgress
4.略	lywè (lyàu)	V/N: to seize, plunder, strategy
侵略	chīnlywè	V/N: invade/encroachment aggression
戰略	jànlywè	N: strategy
5.秘	mì	BF: secret, private
秘密	mìmì	SV: secret, confidential
6.質	jŕ (jr̀)	V/N: to inquire/substance
7.詢	syún (syùn)	V: inquire
詢問	syúnwèn	V: inquire, ask
質詢	jŕsyún	V/N: inquire (in formal sense)/questioning
8.暨	jì	CV: and, together with (The things or persons after <u>jì</u> are always subordinate to the preceding. This is

			the difference between jì on the one hand and gēn, yú, or jí on the other.)
9. 列	lyè	V:	file or rank, to arrange in order
列席	lyè syí	V:	attend a meeting, either as a non-regular member or without vote (cf. chū syí which means "attend (meeting)" or "be present")
10. 繼	jì	V/A:	succeed, continue, subsequently
11. 盡	jìn	V:	to exhaust
詳盡	syángjìn	SV:	exhaustive, detailed
12. 攻	gūng	V:	attack
反攻	fǎngūng	V/N:	counter-attack
13. 復	fù	V/A:	to repeat, recover, furthermore
收復	shōufù	V:	to recover, take back
14. 基	jī	BF:	base
基地	jīdì	N:	a base
基本	jīběn	SV:	basic
15. 胞	pāu	BF:	womb, brethren
同胞	túngpāu	N;	brethren, compatriot

16. 聖	shèng	SV: sacred, holy
神聖	shénshèng	SV: sacred, holy
聖人	shèngren	N: a sage
聖經	shèngjīng	N: the Bible
17. 階	jyē	N: steps (lit.)
階段	jyēdwàn	N: phase, stage
階級	jyējí	N: class (social), (military) rank
18. 配	pèi	V: to match
配合	pèihé	V: to match, be coordinated
19. 俾	bì	V: to enable, to the end that (see Voc. B-22)
20. 際	jì	N: a border, limit
國際	gwójì	BF: international
21. 俄	È (É)	N: Russia
蘇俄	Sūé	N: Soviet Russia

Vocabulary B - New Expressions and Structural Analysis

1. 俞鴻鈞	Yú Húng-jyūn	N: Yú Hung-chün
2. 院	Ywàn	N: Yuan (see Notes)
院長	Ywànjǎng	N: President of Yuan
立法院	Lìfǎywàn	N: Legislative Yuan
立院	Lìywàn	N: abbr. of the above
行政院	Syíngjèngywàn	N: Executive Yuan
院會	Ywànhwèi	N: Yuan meeting (also known as Ywànwù hwèiyì)
3. 施政	shr̄ jèng	VO: administration
4. 盟邦	méngbāng	N: allies, an allied nation (same as ménggwó)
5. 行動	syíngdùng	N/V: action/act, take action
6. 共黨	Gùngdǎng	N: abbr. of Gùngchǎndǎng
7. 主計長	Jǔjìjǎng	N: comptroller-general
8. 財政部	Tsáijèngbù	N: Ministry of Finance
財政部長	Tsáijèngbùjǎng	N: Minister of Finance
9. 年度	nyándù	N: fiscal year
10. 中央政府	jūngyāng jèngfǔ	N: central government
11. 預算	yùswàn	N: budget
總預算案	dzǔngyùswànàn	N: general budget bill

12. 黄國書 Hwáng Gwó-shū N: Huang Kuo-shu

13. 政務委員 jèngwù wěiywán N: member of the Executive Yuan (Ministers without portefolio)

14. 部會 bù hwèi N: ministries and commissions

15. 就施政計劃 jyòu shrjèng jìhwa CV-N: on the programs (or plans) of administration (cf. Selection 9, Voc. B-4)

16. 首…繼… shǒu... jì... at first...and subsequently

17. 龐松舟 Pāng Sūng-jōu N: P'ang Sung-chou, name of an official

18. 徐柏園 Syú Bwó-ywán N: Hsu Po-yüan

19. (對)…加以… (dwèi)...jyāyǐ-V...

The normal word order should be V-N. The transposition of words here with the addition of <u>dwèi</u> makes the N following it definite in nature. <u>jyāyǐ</u> forms a chain of verbal expressions used to introduce the V. (cf. Selection 11, Voc.B-29) Sometimes, <u>yǐ</u> in <u>jyāyǐ</u> may be left out. E.g.

syáng jyā kǎulyù 詳加考慮 to consider carefully

dzài jyā(yǐ) dyàuchá 再加(以)調查 to investigate once more

dwō jyā yántǎu 多加研討 to consider (or examine) carefully

20. 分别 fēnbyé A: separately

21. 解救 jyějyòu V: free, rescue

22. 俾 V　　bì-V

<u>Bì</u>-V forms a chain of verbal expressions, meaning "so as to V" or "thereby V". Fixed expressions with <u>bì</u> include:

俾可	bìkě-V	thereby V, so as to
俾便	bìbyàn-V	so as to (facilitate)
俾使	bìshř	so as to cause (or make)

<u>NOTES</u>

1. The National Government of China 國民政府 is composed of five main branches, namely:

(1) 行政院　　the Executive Yuan

This is the highest executive organ of the Government. It is like a cabinet, and its head corresponds to premier in foreign governments.

(2) 立法院　　the Legislative Yuan

(3) 司法院　　the Judicial Yuan

(4) 考試院　　the Examination Yuan, and

(5) 監察院　　the Control Yuan

Under each Yuan there are ministries and commissions, etc.

2. Since the Republic of China was founded in 1912, the 44th year of the Republic as appearing above, corresponds to the year of 1955.

EXERCISES

I. Translate into English:

1. 詳加解釋
2. 俾便進行
3. 俾可解決
4. 俾使早作準備
5. 分別前往
6. 國民政府共分五院.行政院的工作最重.
7. 立法院明日開會時,將對此事詳加討論.
8. "收復失地"是我們現階段最神聖的責任.

II. Translate into English:

1. 海外同胞
2. 質詢兩小時
3. 廿人出席,五人列席
4. 下年度工作綱要
5. 俾便執行
6. 俾可前往訪問
7. 秘密舉行
8. 反攻中國大陸
9. 國際關係
10. 各部部長
11. 各部會首長
12. 首由財政部長報告

13. 繼由主計長報告

14. 共分四個階段

15. 赴美之前

PART TWO

1. 中華民國政府共有五院,即行政院,立法院,司法院,考試院,監察院。五院之中,行政院最重要;其下設有外交,財政,國防,教育等部。行政院院長與外國政府中總理之地位相同。

2. 據中央日報消息:立法院昨開秘密院會,行政院長暨各部會首長被邀列席。

3. 立法院昨在中山堂舉行秘密會議。首由行政院長報告本年度施政情形。其後,由財政部長對下年度預算之編製經過,作詳盡之說明。最後,立法委員就行政院長與財政部長所作之報告,有所詢問。

4. 行政院院長昨列席立法院會議時稱:台灣為我反攻復國之基地。我們應與盟邦聯合行動,對抗共產國家之侵略,解救大陸上六億同胞。

5. 行政院長並稱:"我們最基本之責任為反共抗俄,收復大陸。"

SELECTION 14

Peking Opera Attracts Wide Attention in Paris

北平京劇團在巴黎演出

法國人喜愛中國古藝術

（紐約時報二日巴黎電）北平國劇團在巴黎之演出，已成爲多年來最受巴黎各界歡迎之一項娛樂。此一劇團係來巴黎參加第二屆國際戲劇藝術慶祝節，據稱，爲一千二百年來首次在國外演出。（按：梅蘭芳前曾在美演出。）至今爲止已二度展延演期。可容二千七百觀衆之劇院每晚滿座。中國戲劇藝術對西洋人雖爲新奇不同，惟極具娛樂性。男女演員穿美麗五彩戲服，歌唱舞蹈。各項不同節目，多係取自長戲中之短段插曲。中國演員之武術，尤使觀衆咋舌。

（紐約聯合日報一九五五年七月八日）

Vocabulary A - New Characters

1. 劇	jyù	N: theatrical plays; opera, drama
京劇	jīngjyù	N: Peking (classical) opera
國劇	gwójyù	N: national opera (Peking opera)
劇團	jyùtwán	N: opera troupe
劇院	jyùywàn	N: opera house
2. 演	yǎn	V: perform, drill
演員	yǎnywán	N: actor, actress
演劇	yǎnjyù	VO: perform a play
3. 藝	yì	N: skill, craft, art
4. 術	shù	N: a device, an artifice
藝術	yìshù	N: arts
美術	měishù	N: fine arts
戰術	jànshù	N: tactics
武術	wǔshù	N: skill with weapons (fencing, etc.)
5. 屆	jyè	M: session, term (conferences, tenure of office, etc.)
		V: arrive (in time), reach
6. 戲	syì	N: plays
戲劇	syìjyù	N: theatrical plays, drama
京戲	jīngsyì	N: Peking opera

7. 延	yán	V: delay, extend
展延	jǎnyán	V: extend
延長	yáncháng	V/N: extend, prolong, lengthen out/extension
8. 衆(眾)	jùng	N: a multitude, a crowd
觀衆	gwānjùng	N: spectators, audience
聽衆	tīngjùng	N: audience
大衆	dàjùng	N: the masses, people
9. 惟	wéi	A: but, nevertheless (interchangeable with the colloq. <u>dànshr</u> or <u>dàn</u>)
10. 麗	lì	SV: beautiful, elegant
美麗	měilì	SV: gorgeous, beautiful
11. 彩	tsǎi	N: hue, color
五彩	wǔtsǎi	N/SV: multicolor/colorful
色彩	sètsǎi	N: color, coloring, tinge
12. 舞	wǔ	V/N: dance
13. 曲	chyǔ	N: ballads
14. 尤	yóu	A: still more, especially

<u>Vocabulary B - New Expressions and Structural Analysis</u>

1. 巴黎	Bālí	PW: Paris
2 娛樂	yúlè	N: amusement, entertainment

3. 按	àn	(editor's)note
4. 梅蘭芳	Méi Lánfāng	N: Mei Lan-fang, a famed actor
5. 至…止	jr̀...jř	up to... (cf. Selection 18, Voc. B-17)
至今為止	jr̀ jīn wéi jř	hitherto, up to now
6. 二度	èrdù	NU-M: (for) two times (cf. Selection 11, Voc. B-5)
7. 容	rúng	V: accommodate
容納	rúngnà	V: accommodate, take (in capacity)
8. 西洋	syīyáng	N: western hemisphere
西洋人	syīyángrén	N: westerners
9. 雖…,惟…	swéi..., wéi...	although...yet (cf. Voc. A-9)
雖…,但…	swéi...,dàn...	
雖…, 然(而)…	swéi..., rán(er)...	
10. 歌唱	gēchàng	N: singing
11. 舞蹈	wǔdǎu	N: dance, folk dance (cf. Voc. A-12)
12. 節目	jyémù	N: program, repertoire
13. 插曲	chāchyǔ	N: episode (cf. Voc. A-13)
14. 咋舌	jà shé	VO: "be flabbergasted", agape, be stunned

EXERCISES

I. Translate into English:

1. 下屆會議
2. 第五屆全體會議(plenary session)
3. 新年即屆
4. 本屆大會
5. 數度
6. 至昨日止
7. 尤受歡迎

II. Translate:

1. 此劇院可容觀衆五千餘人。
2. 京劇亦稱平劇,具有很高之藝術價值.
3. 編者按:此議案將於下屆會議中提出討論.

SELECTION 15

China Petroleum Company Intensifies Efforts on Production

中國石油公司
加緊開採油礦

台北十二日電：中國石油公司爲應中國石油之需要，已經開始加強開採油礦之工作。最近開採之兩個油井，每年出產原油約三千噸。新式採油機器配備已由美國運抵台灣，日內裝置完妥，卽可增加原油產量。同時，關於新油礦之探取，亦正由採礦專家採用美國之新方法，從事空中及地面之科學探測，以期發現更多之油源。

（紐約美洲日報一九五二年六月十三日）

Vocabulary A - New Characters

1.礦	kwàng	N: mines, mineral deposits
油礦	yóukwàng	N: oil deposits
金礦	jīnkwàng	N: gold mines
礦工	kwànggūng	N: mine workers
2.井	jǐng	N: a well
油井	yóujǐng	N: oil well
3.噸	dwūn	M: a ton
4.器	chì	N: tool, utensil
機器	jīchì	N: machine, machinery
5.妥	twǒ	SV: satisfactory, secure
6.探	tàn	V: search out, explore
探取	tànchyǔ	V/N: explore/exploration
偵探	jēntàn	V/N: spy
7.科	kē	N: class or field, science
科學	kēsywé	N: science
8.測	tsè	V: estimate, measure
測量	tsèlyáng	V: measure, survey
測驗	tsèyàn	N/V: test (academic)
9.源	ywán	N: source
來源	láiywán	N: origin
發源	fāywán	V: originate

Vocabulary B - New Expressions and Structural Analysis

1. 石油	shŕyóu	N: petroleum
2. 公司	gūngsz̄	N: company, firm
* 中國石油公司	Jūnggwó Shŕyóu Gūngsz̄	N: China Petroleum Company
3. 加緊	jyājǐn	V: speed up, intensify (effort, etc.)

Jyā is prefaced to certain stative verbs to indicate intensification of a condition. Similar expressions include:

加強	jyāchyáng	V: strengthen, intensify
加深	jyāshēn	V: deepen
加大	jyādà	V: enlarge
加速	jyāsú	V: speed up, expedite

4. 開採	kāitsǎi	V: exploit, open (mines, etc.)
採油	tsǎi yóu	VO: drill (oil, etc.)
5. 為···	wèi...	CV: for the purpose of...
為····起見	wèi.. chǐjyàn	CV: for the purpose of...
為···計	wèi.. jì	CV: for the purpose of... (lit.)

Any of the above expressions serve to form a clause adverbial in nature, and therefore must be placed before the main V in the sentence.

6. 應····需要	yìng...syūyàu	VO: to meet with the need of...

應	yìng	V:	respond (cf. Selection 3, Voc. B-6)
需要	syūyàu	N:	need
7. 出產	chūchǎn	V/N:	produce
8. 原油	ywányóu	N:	crude oil
9. 約	ywē	A:	approximately
大約	dàywē	A:	approximately
10. 配備	pèibèi	V/N:	equip/equipment
11. 日內	r̀nèi	TW:	in a day or so
*12. 裝置	jwāngjr̀	V:	install, set up
13. 產量	chǎnlyàng	N:	output (lit. quantity of production)
大量	dàlyàng	N:	large quantity
14. 家	-jyā	BF:	-ist

Jyā is added to expressions, both nominal and verbal much as the English ending -ist, to denote a specialist in a particular field. E.g.

科學家	kēsywéjyā	N:	scientist (kēsywé, science)
教育家	jyàuyùjyā	N:	educator (jyàuyù, education)
資本家	dzběnjyā	N:	capitalist (dzběn, capital)
專家	jwānjyā	N:	specialist, expert
15. 以期	yǐchī		so as to (expect to)... (cf. Selection 11, Voc. B-21)
16. 從事(於)	tsúngshr̀(yu)	V:	be engaged in

EXERCISES

PART ONE

1. 五彩電影
2. 大約五百噸
3. 約五千人
4. 產量突增
5. 日內即可運到
6. 尤為嚴重
7. 首次在華演出
8. 為應目前之需要計
9. 為加強防務起見
10. 從事於經濟建設
11. 加緊軍事準備
12. 似已測量完妥
13. 我國之光榮
14. 油井頗多
15. 增加石油之出產

PART TWO

1. 關於京戲(或平劇)之來源,說法不一(yi, one, same)有人謂京戲發源於湖北省。有人覺得此種說法不對。我們知道京劇本來是一種地方戲,於一百年前,傳至當時之首都——北京,頗為觀衆所歡迎。

2. 京戲戲服之色彩頗美麗,音樂歌唱尤為觀衆喜愛。其演唱方法復不斷進步。因此,此種藝術早已成為一種全國性之藝術,有時亦稱"國劇"。

3. 我國國劇內容頗豐富(fēngfù, RICH, PLENTIFUL)有的取自我國歷史,亦有根據舊故事而編寫者。國劇除具娛樂性外,常有教育意義。

4. 近數十年以來,國劇界中最有名之演員為梅蘭芳。三十年前,彼曾來美演唱。不幸彼已於一九六一年夏去世。

5. 一九五五年前往巴黎參加國際戲劇節之國劇團中,有李少春,袁世海等演員。彼等復於一九六〇年赴南美各國與加拿大演唱,受到熱烈歡迎。

6. 長江與黃河為我國最長之兩條河,均發源於青海省。長江亦稱揚子江,有三千一百哩之長。黃河長二千七百哩。

7. 中國礦藏(kwàngtsáng, MINERAL DEPOSITS)豐富。例如,金礦、鐵礦、油礦皆多,惟至今開採者頗少。我國以煤(méi, COAL)礦為最多。根據一九八三年之統計,煤之產量為九千九百萬公噸。

8. 近年來,中國加緊工業與農業之生產。據最近官方發表之數字,一九八〇年產鋼(gāng, STEEL)五千八百萬噸。

SELECTION 16

Britain Rejected by Common Market

英欲加入共同市場被拒

甘廼迪檢討歐洲新情勢

（路透社布魯塞爾一月廿九日電）英國申請加入西歐共同市場，今日以法國否決，未能成功。

共同市場談判破裂。六個會員國宣佈獲致協議已不可能。

（台北中央日報中華民國五十二年一月三十日）

（路透社羅馬二月三日電）英首相

麥克米倫今天午後離此飛返倫敦。渠頃對記者談話，強調歐洲團結之重要。

（中央社華盛頓二日法新電）今日獲悉，甘廼迪總統今晨與美國駐英大使會談，檢討英國參加共同市場失敗後之歐洲情勢。

（中央社紐約二日合衆國際電）甘廼迪總統之貿易特別顧問赫特今天由羅馬返國。據說，彼攜有打破歐洲僵局之經濟建議。

（台北中央日報中華民國五十二年二月四日）

（華盛頓訊）此間外交界人士稱，戴高樂政府

之所以否決英國加入共同市場，原因尚未完全明白・惟一家報紙認為，法國政府此舉或因不欲英國勢力進入歐洲大陸之故・

Vocabulary A - New Characters

1. 拒	jyù	V:	reject, refuse
拒絶	jyùjywé	V/N:	reject/refusal
2. 申	shēn	BF:	notify, explain
申請	shēnchǐng	V:	apply for
3. 裂	lyè	V:	crack, split
破裂	pwòlyè	V:	be broken, be broken down
4. 協	syé	BF:	aid, harmonize
協議	syéyì	N:	agreement, mutual consent
協助	syéjù	V/N:	aid
5. 渠	chyú	PN:	he (literary)
6. 貿	màu	BF:	trade
貿易	màuyì	N:	trade
7. 顧	gù	V:	care for
顧問	gùwèn	N:	adviser
8. 攜(携)	syé (syī)	V:	carry, take with
9. 僵	jyāng	SV:	be stiff
僵局	jyāngjyú	N:	deadlock
10. 士	shr̀	N:	gentry, scholar, warrior
人士	rénshr̀	N:	persons (of rank or social distinction)

11. 尚	shàng	A:	still, yet (a literary word interchangeable with the colloq. hai)

Vocabulary B - New Expressions and Structural Analysis

1. 加入	jyārù	V:	join (in a group)
2. 共同市場	Gùngtúng Shr̀chǎng	N:	Common Market
共同	gùngtúng	BF:	common
市場	shr̀chǎng	N:	Market
3. 甘迺迪	Gānnǎidí	N:	Kennedy
4. 布魯塞爾	Bùlǔsàiěr	PW:	Brussels
5. 否決	fǒujywé	V:	veto
6. 談判	tánpàn	V/N:	negotiate/talks
7. 獲致	hwòjr̀	V:	attain, reach (an agreement)
8. 羅馬	Lwómǎ	PW:	Rome
9. 首相	shǒusyàng	N:	prime minister
10. 麥克米倫	Màikèmǐlwún	N:	Macmillan
11. 倫敦	Lwúndwūn	PW:	London
12. 強調	chyángdyàu	V:	state emphatically
13. 團結	twánjye	V/N:	unite/bond, alliance
14. 法新(社)電	Fǎsyīn(shè) dyàn		A dispatch by the Agence France Presse

15. 赫特 Hètè N: Herter

16. 戴高樂 Dàigāulè N: De Gaulle

17. N之所以V,原因是.... the reason why N + V is ..

N之所以V,係因.... ditto

N之所以V,原因在於....the reason why N + V lies in ...

18. 大陸 dàlù N: mainland

19. 因....之故 yīn ... jīgù because of the reason ... (interch. with the colloq. yīnwei .... de ywángu)

EXERCISES

PART ONE

1. 尚未公佈
2. 尚有可能
3. 頃已離此
4. 將成僵局
5. 教育界人士
6. 強調此點
7. 因此之故
8. 攜有重要文件
9. 國際貿易問題
10. 軍事顧問數人

PART TWO

1. 西歐共同市場包括法國,西德,義大利,比利時,荷蘭,盧森堡六國。

2. 共同市場對英國申請參加一事,談判甚久,惟至今尚無協議。

3. 法國否决英國參共同市場,西歐因此已成僵局。

4. 法國政府為何 (hé, WHAT) 反對英國加入共同市場,原因尚未獲悉.

5. 戴高樂政府之所以反對英國加入共同市場,據此間人士稱,或係不欲英國勢力進入歐洲大陸。

SELECTION 17

Britain Holds General Election

英定五月廿六日舉行普選

二黨競爭將以遠東爲主題

（美聯社十六日倫敦電）英國首相艾登昨晚宣佈英國普選將於五月二十六日舉行。此次保守勞工二黨之競選，將着重於經濟方面之貿易問題與遠東問題二要題。勞工黨領袖批評艾登之迅速宣佈普選日期，實因國内經濟狀況已趨惡化之故。同時，勞工黨並批評當政之保守黨至最近始有意促開強國會議，解決世界問題。艾登昨日在無線電台廣播，稱內閣將於五月六日解散，以等候廿六日之普選。新內閣將於七月七日組成云。

（紐約聯合日報一九五五年四月十八日）

塔斯社評論

英大選保守黨獲勝

聯合社莫斯科廿八日電：蘇聯官方通訊社今日就英國大選結果發表評論，指出保守黨之所以獲得勝利，主要原因在於該黨以舉行四國首長會議作爲諾言。

塔斯社說，倫敦的政治觀察家認爲：保守黨勝利的主要因素是因爲該黨的領袖們在競選演講中表示願意緩和國際緊張局勢和舉行大國談判解決國際問題。

（紐約華僑日報一九五五年五月三十日）

Vocabulary A - New Characters

1.競	jìng	V:	to strive, emulate
競爭	jìngjēng	V/N:	compete/competition
競選	jìngsywǎn	V/N:	campaign (election)
2.貿	màu	BF:	trade
貿易	màuyì	N:	trade
3.評	píng	V:	criticize, discuss
批評	pīpíng	V/N:	criticize/criticism
評論	pínglwùn	V/N:	comment/comment, commentary
4.迅	syìn	SV/A:	quick, hasty
迅速	syìnsú	SV/A:	prompt/ speedily
5.況	kwàng	N:	condition
狀況	jwàngkwàng	N:	condition, circumstances
況且	kwàngchyě	MA:	moreover
6.趨	chyū	V:	to hasten
趨勢	chyūshr̀	N:	trend, tendency
7.惡	è (wù)	SV:	evil, wicked
惡化	è hwà	N:	to worsen (cf. Selection 14, Voc. B-12)
惡感	ègǎn	N:	ill-feelings
8.促	tsù	V:	to urge, press
9.閣	gé	N:	cabinet (government)
內閣	nèigé	N:	cabinet

*10.諾	nwò	V:	answer, promise
* 諾言	nwòyán	N:	a promise, a pledge
11.素	sù	N/A:	element/ordinarily
因素	yīnsù	N:	factor
平素	píngsù	A:	ordinarily
12.緩	hwǎn	SV:	slow (lit.)
緩和	hwǎnhé	V:	to ease

Vocabulary B - New Expressions and Structural Analysis

1.選舉	sywǎnjyǔ	V/N:	vote, elect/election
普選	pǔsywǎn	N:	general election
大選	dàsywǎn	N:	general election
2.以⋯⋯為⋯⋯	yǐ...wéi		to take...as (or to be)...
*3.主題	jǔtí	N:	main issue
要題	yàutí	N:	main issue
4.倫敦	Lwúndwūn	PW:	London
5.首相	shǒusyàng	N:	prime minister (shǒu, head, chief, first)
6.保守黨	Bǎushǒudǎng	N:	Conservative Party
保守	bǎushǒu	SV:	conservative

7. 勞工黨 Láugūngdǎng
N: Labor Party

工黨 Gūngdǎng N: Labor Party

8. 着重 jwójùng V: emphasize, stress

9. ⋯方面 ...fāngmyàn
N: aspect, field, respect

<u>Fāngmyàn</u> commonly follows a N, meaning "in the field of N" or simply "in N". E.g.

(在)政治方面 (dzài) jèngjr̀ fāngmyàn
in the field of politics

(在)農業方面 (dzài) núngyè fāngmyàn
in the field of agriculture

在這方面 dzài jè fāngmyàn
in this respect

Compare "...<u>fāngmyàn</u>", which is a N, with "... <u>shàng</u>", which is a boundform. E.g.

(在)政治上 (dzài) jèngjr̀shàng
in politics/political, politically

10. 因⋯之故 yīn...jr̄ gù
because of the reason...(lit.)

11. 當政 dāngjèng VO: in (political) power

當權 dāngchywán
VO: in power (<u>chywán</u>, authority)

12. 始 shř A: then, then only (interchangeable with the colloq. <u>tsái</u>)

13. 強國 chyánggwó N: powers, powerful nations

五強	Wǔ Chyáng	N:	Five Powers
14. 解散	jyěsàn	V/N:	disperse, dissolve/ dispersal
15. 就N, V....	jyòu N, V...		with respect to or concerning N, V...

Jyòu is a CV, bringing a N before a V. (cf. Selection 9, Voc. B- 4)

16. N之所以V...,原因是... — the reason why N ≠ V..., is/../that N ≠ V... is because...

N之所以V...,原因在於.... — the reason why N ≠ V... lies in (the fact that)...

N之所以V...,是因為.... — that N ≠ V ... is because...

17. 觀察家	gwānchájyā	N:	observer
觀察	gwānchá	V/N:	observe/observations
18. 認為	rènwéi	V:	be of opinion, hold (opinion)
19. 談判	tánpàn	V/N:	negotiate/negotiation (cf. Selection 15, Voc. A-13)

NOTES

1. The primary purpose of this Selection is to provide students with vocabulary commonly used in connection with Britain's government and politics.

EXERCISES

I. Discuss the politics and governmental structure of Britain, using the vocabulary employed here.

II. Make sentences with:

1. 因……之故
2. ……之所以……，是因為……
3. 雖……，惟……

III. Translate:

1. 他昨日之所以未去，係因工作太忙之故.
2. 他在其競選演說中，着重經濟改革.

IV. Translate the present Selection into English:

SELECTION 18

U.S. Senate Extends Draft Law for Four Years; Eisenhower Urges Congress to Pass Military Reserve Bill

參議院通過延長徵兵法四年
艾森豪促國會通過後備兵法

合衆社美京十七日訊：聯邦參院頃於昨晚通過延長徵兵法有效期間四年。參院軍事委員會主席羅素參議員稱，此爲美國全部國防之基礎。渠並表示，如目前冷戰狀態繼續存在，該項徵兵法將再延長十年至廿年，甚至更長之期間，俾使美國之實力得以保持強大。該法案前已經衆院通過，但參院對該法案復提出修正案兩項，尚須送衆院通過，然後再送白宮，由艾森豪總統簽署後，始能生效。

又訊：參院軍事委員會頃決議，暫將艾森豪總統所提強制後備兵訓練法停止討論。……。又艾森豪總統防空演習後向全美人士呼籲，促國會立卽通過該法，以充實美國軍備，而避免原子戰爭之發生云。

Vocabulary A - New Characters

1.延	yán	BF:	extend (cf. Selection 19, Voc. A-7)
延長	yáncháng	V:	extend
2.徵	jēng	V:	to levy, recruit (troops); solicit
徵兵	jēng bīng	VO:	to enlist under conscription; draft
徵兵法	jēngbīngfǎ	N:	Draft Bill; Military Conscription Law
徵求	jēngchyóu	V:	to solicit, seek for
徵收	jēngshōu	V:	to levy and collect, as taxes
3.頃	chǐng	TW:	just now, a short while ago (lit.)
4.礎	chǔ	BF:	foundation, basis
基礎	jīchǔ	N:	foundation, basis
5.渠	chyú	PN:	he (lit.)
渠等	chyúděng	PN:	they, them (lit.)
6.態	tài	N:	manner, bearing
狀態	jwàngtài	N:	conditions, circumstances
態度	tàidù	N:	attitude
7.尚	shàng	A:	still, yet (interchangeable with the colloq. <u>hái</u>)
8.宮	gūng	N:	palace
白宮	Báigūng	N:	White House

9. 署	shǔ	N: a public office
署名	shǔ míng	VO: to sign (one's name)
簽署	chyānshǔ	V: to sign (one's name)
10. 士	shr̀	N: gentlemen, warrior, scholar
人士	rénshr̀	N: people (of rank or distinction)

a. 社會人士 b. 教育界人士

11. 籲	yù	V: to appeal
呼籲	hūyù	V: to appeal, plead
籲請	yùchǐng	V: to plead
12. 避	bì	V: avoid
避免	bìmyǎn	V: avoid

<u>Vocabulary B - New Expressions and Structural Analysis</u>

1. 參議院	Tsānyìywàn	N: Senate (U. S.)
參院	Tsānywàn	N: Senate
參議員	Tsānyìywán	N: senator
上院	Shàngywàn	N: House of Lords (Britain), upper house
2. 衆議院	Jùngyìywàn	N: House of Representatives
衆院	Jùngywàn	N: House of Representatives

	衆議員	Jùngyìywán	N:	House of Representatives
	下院	Syàywàn	N:	House of Commons (Britain), lower house
3.	國會	Gwóhwèi	N:	Congress, Parliament
*4.	後備兵法	Hòubèibīngfǎ	N:	Military Reserve Bill
	後備兵	hòubèibīng	N:	reserve troops
5.	聯邦	lyánbāng	N:	federation, federal government
*6.	羅素	Lwósù	N:	Russell
7.	使…得以	shř...déyǐ ∤ V		to enable (to cause... to be able)
*8.	修正案	syōujèngàn	N:	amendment
	修正	syōujèng	V/N:	revise, correct/ revision
9.	決議	jywéyì	V:	to resolve, decide
	決議案	jywéyìàn	N:	a resolution (passed at a meeting)
	議決	yìjywé	V:	to resolve, to pass a resolution
*10.	強制	chyángjr̀	SV:	compulsory
11.	演習	yǎnsyí	N/V:	maneuver, drill (military)
12.	立即	lìjì	A:	immediately, instantly (cf. Selection 11, Voc. A-3)
13.	充實	chūngshŕ	V:	strengthen, to make full

14. 軍備 jyūnbèi N: armament (bèi for pèibèi)

15. 以…而… yǐ ∤ V...ér ∤ V... in order to...and (moreover)...

16. 原子 ywándž N: atom

NOTES

1. This Selection is designed, among other reasons, to provide students with vocabulary of American government and politics.

EXERCISES

I. Discuss the politics and governmental structure of the United States.

II. Translate:

1. 美國參議院有參議員一百人. 在第九十二屆國會中,衆議院有衆議員四百三十五人.
2. 英國國會分上院下院二院.

SELECTION 19

Advertisements and Public Announcements

(一)

吉房招租

現有新房一所出租水電全交通
便近菜市杭州南路一〇五巷卄五號

住宅廉讓

交通便設備全四間南海
路二巷十二弄九號

(二)

孫明三長子
爲
高文成次女

結婚啓事

謹定於中華
民國七十四

年八月二日假中山路光華飯店舉行結婚典禮
特此敬告
諸親友

(三)

國立西北大學校友會啓事
茲訂於本(三)月十六日(星期日)下午二時假台北
漢口街一段糖業公司會議室召開會員大會敬希
旅台
諸仁友屆時撥冗出席爲荷

Vocabulary A - New Characters

I.

1.吉	jí	SV:	auspicious, lucky (lit.)
2.租	dzū	V:	rent
出租	chūdzū	V:	to let (for rent)
招租	jāudzū	V:	to let (for rent)
3.巷	syàng	N:	alley, lane
4.宅	jái	N:	residence, dwelling
住宅	jùjái	N:	residence
5.廉	lyán	SV/A:	reasonable in price/ cheaply (lit.)

II.

6.謹	jǐn	SV/A:	cautious, respectful/ respectfully

III.

7.茲	dž	TW:	now, here, this (lit.)
茲因	dž yīn		now because (of)...
8.糖	táng	N:	sugar, candy
糖業	tángyè	N:	sugar industry
9.仁	rén	SV:	virtuous (lit.)
*10.撥	bwō	V:	to allot, transfer (as money), to make appropriations

Vocabulary B - New Expressions and Structural Analysis

I.

1.菜市	tsàishr̀	N: vegetable market
市場	shr̀chǎng	N: market
*2.杭州南路	Hángjōu Nán Lù	PW: S. Hongchow Avenue
3.讓	ràng	V: cede, sell
4.間	jyān	M: for rooms
*5.南海路	Nánhǎi Lù	PW: Nanhai Avenue
*6.弄	nùng (lùng)	N: small alley

II.

7.啟事	chǐshr̀	N: a notice
*8.孫明三	Swūn Míng-sān	N: a fictitious name
*9.高玉成	Gāu Yù-chéng	N: a fictitious name
10.長	jǎng	V/SV: to grow/senior
長子	jǎngdž̌	N: the eldest son
長女	jǎngnyǔ	N: the eldest daughter
11.次	tsž̀	SV: second, next
次女	tsž̀nyǔ	N: the second daughter
次日	tsž̀nr̀	TW: the next day
12.假	jyǎ	V: borrow, avail of
*13.光華飯店	Gwānghwá Fàndyàn	N: Kwanghwa Restaurant

14. 特此…… tètsž (≠ V) It is hereby to...

This is a closing phrase in a notice.

III.

*15. 國立西北大學 Gwólì Syīběi Dàsywé N: National Northwestern University

16. 校友會 syàuyǒuhwèi N: alumni association

校友 syàuyǒu N: alumnus, alumna

*17. 漢口街 Hànkǒu Jyē PW: Hankou Street

18. 屆時 jyèshŕ TW: then, at that time (when the time comes)

*19. 撥冗 bwō rúng VO: put one's multifarious affairs aside, to take time out

20. 敬希……為荷 jìng syī...wéihé

(I) respectfully hope (that you will do such and such) and shall appreciate it. A closing phrase.

Similar phrases include:

....為盼 ...wéipàn ...be obliged

....為感 ...wéi gǎn ...be grateful

NOTES

It is to be expected that Chinese advertisements and public notices, like their English counterparts, will be brief and pithy in style. They differ however in not having punctuation, a characteristic derived from classical Chinese.

PART ONE

1. 廉價出賣
2. 住宅區
3. 我國旅美人士
4. 希屆時出席
5. 其長子頃已啓程
6. 訂於下週歸國
7. 國立北京大學校友會
8. 假中山公園舉行
9. 吉房召租啓事
10. 茲有住宅一所廉讓
11. 敬希屆時參加為荷
12. 特此敬告　諸親友

ADDITIONAL ARTICLES

The following four articles, all adopted from recent newspapers, are annotated somewhat differently from the preceding texts. First of all, the vocabulary glosses are listed in consecutive order as they occur in the article. There is no division between New Characters (Vocabulary A) and New Expressions (Vocabulary B) as in earlier lessons. Structural analysis is kept to a minimum. All annotations are by word unit rather than by single character.

This group of four articles are followed by others without annotations. We include these new articles so that the student can try out his new skills without the aid of glosses. To do so will usually require consulting a Chinese-English dictionary. One good one now available is the PINYIN CHINESE-ENGLISH DICTIONARY, compiled by the staff at the Beijing Language Institute. You can purchase this dictionary from a variety of sources, including Far Eastern Publications. Since this dictionary was originally published in China, it naturally employs Hanyu Pinyin romanization and, of course, is printed in simplified characters. So some adjustment is necessary. Another helpful dictionary in unsimplified characters is the NEW PRACTICAL CHINESE-ENGLISH DICTIONARY, published in Taiwan (also available from Far Eastern Publications).

Selection Twenty

Over Forty Countries Send Students to China For Study

歐美四十多個國家
派遣學生來粵留學
多數選學漢語也有學習中醫

（香港廿五日專電）廣州消息：據記者從有關方面獲悉，近年來廣東省各高等院校共接受了四十多個國家和地區的二百多人來粵留學。人數之多，地區之廣，都是前所未有的。

據悉，其中美國、西德、新西蘭、澳大利亞、西班牙、瑞典、南斯拉夫等國，還是首次派留學生來粵留學的。

在這些外國留學生當中，他們多數選學漢語，也有學習中醫、針灸、蠶桑技術和法律的，學習年限短者三兩月，長者六年。來粤留學生中，有些已學成歸國。目前仍在省内各高等學府學習的還有七十五人。

Vocabulary

歐美	Oū-Měi	N: (shortened form) Europe and (North) America; Western countries
中美	Jūng-Měi	China and the United States
派遣	pàichyǎn	V: send; dispatch
留學	lyóusywé	V: study overseas
留學生	lyóuywésheng	foreign student
選	sywǎn	V: choose; select
學習	sywésyí	N/V: study
中醫	Jūng-yī	N: (shortened form) Chinese medicine
中國醫學		Jūnggwo yīsywé
消息	syāusyi	N: news; tidings
據	jyù	CV: according to; on the grounds of
據我看	jyù wǒ kàn	as I see it; in my opinion
據我所知	jyù wǒ sǔo jr̄	as far as I know
从…獲息	tsúng ... hwòsyī	(literary) it is learned from ...
高等	gāuděng	Att: higher
高等學校	gāuděng sywésyàu	institution of higher learning
學院	sywéywàn	N: (educational) institute

共	gùng	A:	(shortened form) altogether (yigung)
接受	jyēshòu	V:	accept
接受意見	jyēshòu yìjian		take advice
前所未有	chyánswǒwèiyǒu		unprecedented; hitherto unknown
據息	jyùsyī		(literary) it is reported
其中	chíjūng		among (the preceding)
西德	Syī-Dé	N:	West Germany
新西蘭	Syīn Syīlán	N:	New Zealand
澳大利亞	Àudàlìyǎ	N:	Australia
西班牙	Syībānyǎ	N:	Spain
瑞典	Rwèidyǎn	N:	Sweden
南斯拉夫	Nánszlāfū	N:	Yugoslavia
在…當中	dzài ... dāngjūng		among ...
針灸	jēnjyǒu	N:	acupuncture and moxibustion
蠶桑	tsánsāng	N:	silkworm
技術	jìshù	N:	technique; skill; technology
年限	nyánsyàn	N:	number of years fixed (for
歸國	gwēigwó		return to (one's) country
目前	mùchyán	TW:	at present; now; presently
仍	réng	A:	still
仍然	réngrán	A;	still; yet

Selection Twenty-one

Reagan Concludes European Visit
Desires Meeting with Gorbachev

里根結東訪歐
强調願會戈氏
西方觀察說收穫不多

（新華社里斯本五月十一日電）美國總統里根十日在葡萄牙首都里斯本再次强調說，他願意會見蘇聯領導人戈爾巴喬夫。里根在結束為期十天對西德、西班牙、法國、葡萄牙四國之行回國前在里斯本機場向記者發表講話時說這番話的。里根說，美蘇兩國「有很多可談的東西」。他認爲，美蘇雙方現在「是開始會談的時候而不是各自談論對方的時了」。

里根是在歐洲議會發表講話後於八日抵達里斯本的。在葡萄牙訪問期間，里根分別會見了葡萄牙總統埃亞内斯和總理蘇亞雷斯，並同蘇亞雷斯着重就東西方關係、葡萄牙即將加入歐洲共同體、美國向葡萄牙提供軍援、中美洲和南部非洲、莫桑比克以及安哥拉局勢等問題舉行了會談。

Vocabulary

里根	Lǐgēn	(Ronald) Reagan
結束	jyéshù	N/V: end; finish; wind up; conclude; close
結束講話	jyéshù jyǎnghwà	wind up a speech
没有結束	méiyou jyéshù	there is no end/endless
訪	fǎng	V: visit; call on
訪友	fǎng yóu	call on a friend
訪問	fǎngwèn	visit; interview
強調	chyángdyàu	V: stress; emphasize; underline
願	ywàn	V: (shortened form) desire; want (ywànyì)
願意	ywànyì	
會	hwèi	N/V: (shortened form) meeting; to meet (with)
歡迎會	hwānyíng hwèi	welcoming meeting
會見	hwèijyàn	meet with (esp. with a foreign visitor)
會客	hwèikè	meet with a guest
戈	Gē	N: (abbreviation) Ge'erbachyaufu Gorbachev (Mikhail S. Gorbachev, leader of Soviet Union
戈爾巴喬夫		
氏	-shr̀	family name
張氏兄弟	Jāngshì syūngdì	The Jang brothers

观察	gwānchá	V: observe N: (shortened form) observer
观察員	gwāncháywán	observer
收穫	shōuhwò	N/V results; gains; harvest; to harvest/gather in (the crop)
里斯本	Lǐszběn	N: Lisbon
葡萄牙	Pútáuyǎ	N: Portugal
再次	dzàitsz	A: once more; a second time; once again
再三	dzàisān	A; over and over again
領導	lǐngdǎu	V: to lead: exercise leadership
領導人	lǐngdǎurén	N: leader
會見	hwèijyàn	V: to meet with
為期	wéichī	(to be completed) by a definite date
會議為期三天	hwèiyì wéichī sāntyān	The meeting will last three days
行	-syíng	travel; trip
非洲之行	Fēijōu jr syíng	A trip to Africa
四國之行	szgwó jr syíng	A four-nation trip
機場	jīchǎng	N: airport
番	-fān	M: (for times, occasions, similar in usage to -tsz, -hwei)
各自	gèdz	P: each; respective; individual

談論	tánlwùn	V: talk about; discuss
對方	dwèifāng	N: the other side
各自談論對方	gedz̀ tánlwùn dwèifāng	each of us talk about the other side
議會	yìhwèi	N: parliament; legislative assembly
埃亞內斯	Āiyǎnèisz̄	(name of the President of Portugal)
蘇亞雷斯	Sūyǎlèisz̄	(name of Prime Minister of Portugal)
着重	jwójùng	V: stress; emphasize
就…問題	jyòu ... wèntí	on the question(s) of ...)
東西方關係	dūng-syīfāng gwānsyi	East-West relations
即將	jíjyāng	A: be about to; be on the point of
加入	jyārù	V: join; accede to
加入條約	jyārù tyáuywē	accede to a treaty
歐洲共同體	Oūjōu Gùngtúng Tǐ	N: The European (Economic) Community
提供	tígūng	V: provide; supply; furnish; offer
軍援	jyūnywán	N: military aid
中美洲	Jūng-Měijōu	N: Central America
莫桑比克	Mwòsāngbǐkē	N: Mozambique
安哥拉	Āngēlā	N: Angola
局勢	jyúshr̀	N: situation;

Selection Twenty-Two

Deng Xiaoping Calls "Open Door Policy" Beneficial To World Peace

鄧小平稱開放政策
有利於世界上和平
贏得朋友·加速發展

（中新文化社香港十七日電）據中國新聞社北京消息：中共中央顧問委員會主任鄧小平今天上午在會見比利時首相馬爾滕斯時說，一個强大的歐州，一個强大的中國，是制約戰爭，維護世果和平的重要力量。

鄧小平說，已故毛澤東主席、周恩來總理和我本人都是强大的、聯合的歐洲的贊助者、熱心人。世界和平與安全需要一個強大的、聯合的歐洲。在當前國際形勢下，歐洲只有聯合，否則沒有別的出路。當然這是一件非常困難又非常複雜的事，但是可以小步前進。

鄧小平指出，中國的發展主要靠自己，但是也要靠朋友。他說，爲什麼我們制訂對外開放政策？就是爲了贏得朋友，加速自己的發展。這不僅是從中國本身利益考慮，而且是從爭取世界持久和平的戰略角度考慮的。

Vocabulary

鄧小平	Dēng Syǎupíng	N: Deng Xiaoping
稱	chēng	V: say; state (lit.)
開放	kāifàng	SV: open (to outside influence, to traffic, to public use)
開放政策	kāifàng jèngtsè	(China's) "Open Door Poicy"
有利	yǒulì	SV: advantageous; beneficial; favorable
有利於	yǒulìyú	be beneficial to (yú)
贏得	yíngdé	V: win; gain; attain
加速	jyāsù	V: quicken; speed up; accelerate; expedite
顧問	gùwèn	N: advisor; consultant
顧問委員會	gùwèn wěiywánhwèi	advisory committee
比利時	Bǐlìshŕ	N: Belgium
首相	shǒusyàng	N: Prime Minister
馬爾滕斯	Mǎěrtàisz̄	(name of Prime Minister of Belgium)
強大	chyángdà	SV: strong; powerful; formidable
制約	jr̀ywē	V: restrict
已故	yǐgù	Att: deceased; late
贊助	dzànjù	N: support; assistance

熱心	rèsyīn	SV: ardent; enthusiastic
當前	dāngchyán	TW: present; current
形勢	syíngshr̀	N: situation; circumstances
否則	fǒudzé	A: otherwise; if not; or else
出路	chūlù	N: way out; outlet
小步	syǎubù	N: small step; half step
前進	chyánjìn	IV: advance; forge ahead
指出	jřchū	V: indicate; point out; refer to
主要	jǔyàu	A: main; chief; principal; major
制訂	jr̀dìng	V: work out; map out; formulate
不僅	bùjǐn	A; not only
本身	běnshēn	A: itself; in itself
利益	lìyì	N: interest; benefit; profit
考慮	kǎulyù	V: consider; think over
爭取	jēngchyǔ	V: strive for; struggle for
持久	chŕjyǒu	SV: lasting; enduring; protracted
角度	jyǎudù	N: angle; point of view

Selection Twenty-Three

Dalai Lama In Interview States Life in Tibet Shows Improvement

達賴在報章發表談話稱
西藏生活獲得改善
漢人態度比前更好

（法新社新德里二十日電）在印度流亡的西藏人精神領袖達賴喇嘛說中國的生活情況有改善。今天這裡的報章引用他的話指出，在北京的統治下，西藏的物質生活有改善，許多西藏人被任命爲軍官。達賴還說，漢人對西藏人的態度比過去更好。達賴週一在東比合爾省佛教中心波特卡對記者發表上述講話。據報導，他回顧過去西藏人生活在飢餓之中，現在食物情況好轉，雖然貧困仍然存在。

不久以前，達賴曾經表示過當西藏人民對他們的生活感到滿意時，他準備回到西藏。過去三年來，流亡在海外的西藏人有一百七十八人返回中國定居，另七百六十人回去訪問。

Vocabulary

達賴	Dá-lài	Dalai (Lama)
報章	bàujāng	N: newspaper
獲得	hwòdé	V: gain; attain; win
改善	gǎishàn	V/N: improve; improvement
流亡	lyóuwáng	go into exile
流亡政府	lyóuwáng jèngfǔ	government-in-exile
精神領袖	jīngshen lǐngsyòu	N: spiritual leader
達賴喇嘛	Dá-lài Lā-ma	Dalai Lama
引用	yǐnyùng	V: quote; cite
統治	tǔngjr̀	V/N: to control; control; domination
物質	wùjr̀	N: material; matter
被..V..為...	bèi.V.wéi...	be VERBED as ...
任命	rènmìng	V: appoint
任命他為校長	rènmìng tā wèi syàujǎng	appoint him as (school) president
比合爾	Bǐhé'ěr shěng	N: Bihar state (India)
佛教	fwójyàu	N: Buddhism
波特卡	Bwōtèkǎ	(place in Bihar state, India)
上述	shàngshù	above-mentioned; aforementioned
達到上述目標	dádàu shàngshù mùbyāu	achieve the above-mentioned objectives

回顧	hwéigù	V/N: look back at; review; recall; recollection
1977年的回顧	yījyǒuchīchīnyán de hwéigù	1977 in retrospect
飢餓	jīè	N: hunger; starvation
在飢餓之中	dzài jīè jr̄ jūng	in the (depths) of hunger/deprivation
食物	shŕwù	N: foodstuff; provisions; food; edibles
好轉	hǎujwǎn	IV: take a turn for the better; improve
形勢好轉	chíngshr̀ hǎujwǎn	the situation improved
貧困	pínkwùn	SV/N: poor; impoverished; poverty
生活貧困	shēnghwǒ pínkwùn	live in poverty
存在	tswúndzài	V: exist; be
曾經	tséngjīng	A: already
表示	byǎushr̀	V: show; express; indicate
滿意	mǎnyì	V/N: satisfied; pleased; satisfaction
返	fǎn(hwéi)	V: return
定居	dìngjyū	IV: settle down; take up residence
另	lìng	P: another; other; separate
另有打算	lìng yǒu dǎswàn	have other plans
另想办法	lìng syǎng bànfǎ	find some other way

Selection Twenty-Four

趙紫陽總理舉行盛大招待會
慶祝建國三十五週年
胡耀邦、趙紫陽、李先念等同西哈努克親王和夫人等五大洲賓客出席

（新華社三十日電）國慶節前夕——九月三十日晚，國務院總理趙紫陽在人民大會堂舉行盛大招待會，慶祝中華人民共和國建國三十五週年。

七時十五分，趙紫陽總理偕同胡耀邦

總書記，李先念主席，彭眞委員長，以及應邀參加我國國慶典禮的各國代表團的主要貴賓們一起步入宴會大廳。這時全體起立，暴風雨般的掌聲響徹全場。

在主席臺前的貴賓們有：民主柬埔寨主席西哈努克親王和夫人，贊比亞總統卡翁達的夫人，國際奧委會主席薩馬蘭奇和夫人。

招待會由趙紫陽總理主持。招待會開始，樂隊奏起莊嚴的中華人民共和國國歌。

中華人民共和國國務院總理趙紫陽在招待會上作了慶祝中華人民共和國建國三十五週年的講話。他的講話不斷獲得全場熱烈的掌聲。

交談。招待會始終洋溢着團結，友好的熱烈氣氛。

接着，黨和國家領導人向中外來賓頻頻祝酒，親切

出席招待會的共有二千多人。

（人民日報一九八四年十月一日）

Selection Twenty-five

中國人口逾十億八百萬
有關資料即將出版
共七卷三十多萬個數據

（新華社北京一月三十一日電）一套中國統計史上最準確、最豐富的人口資料表明，截至一九八二年七月一日零時，中國大陸二十九個省、自治區、直轄市的總人口爲十億零八百一十八萬零七百三十八人。

這套統計資料是中國第一次使用電子計算機處理龐大的人口普查資料而獲得的

。全部資料共編爲七卷。它提供了人口地區分佈、民族、年齡、文化程度、行業和職業、家庭與婚姻、生育狀況等方面的三十多萬個數據。這套資料將於今年上半年由中國統計出版社出版，向國內外公佈。它將爲中國研究人口和社會經濟問題、制定政策和編制計劃提供重要依據，爲世界人口統計和人口研究作出重要的貢獻。

Selection Twenty-six

北京美國電影節
市民愛看金池塘

（美聯社北京一日電）被「星際戰爭」裡的外星人所迷惑，但給「礦工的女兒」及「金池塘」這兩部人性的電影吸引的中國人，週一塞滿了北京二十九家播映五部獲得奧斯卡金像獎的戲院。

在中國首次舉行的美國電影節的電影票，均已售空。電影節中除了上述三部電影外，還播映「克拉瑪對抗克拉瑪」及「轉捩點」兩部名片。

爲了應付廣大的觀衆，有些電影院的放映時間，提早到破曉以前。許多沒有買到票的人，站在票房外面，揮動着鈔票，想要買退票。有些人説，他們願意付出五十分一張票的五倍的價錢，來購買退票。由中國文化部選擇並注上中文字幕的五部美國片子，將從今日至十四日在五個城市播映，預計將有兩千萬觀衆觀賞。這是中美正式的文化交流。

1. 現在我們已將讀報入門念完。此書共二十餘課。其中有國內新聞，亦有國外及國際新聞。

2. 以新聞性質而言，此書有政治新聞，有軍事新聞，亦包括經濟文化等方面之新聞。

3. 以新聞來源而論，此書不僅有中央社新華社所發之消息，並有美聯國際社路透社塔斯社等外國通訊社之新聞。

4. 惟本書僅二百頁，係一"入門"性質之讀物。除新聞廿餘條與廣告數條之外，未能有一二社論，至為可惜。

5. 我們對於世界局勢，對於中國各項問題，皆應隨時注意。因此，我們應常看中文報紙。

6. 各位讀者現對中文已具相當基礎。本書作者謹以至誠 (jr̀chéng, UTMOST SINCERITY) 希望諸位讀者繼續努力，不斷進步。

GLOSSARY

1-3 Strokes

之	jr̄ of, x's	p	27
之一	jr̄ yī one of ...	ph	137
一度	yīdù at one time, formerly	tw	121
一日	yīr̀ first day (of a month)/one day	nu/n	17
一般	yìbān alike, like	cv	59
二度	èrdù (for) two times	nu-m	156
已	yǐ already	a	16
已故	yǐgù deceased; late	att	207
七十	chīshŕ seven o'clock	n	39
下機	syàjī get off an airplane	vo	135
下院	Syàywàn House of Commons	n	186
士	shr̀ gentry, scholar, warrior	n	169
大臣	dàchén minister, high minister	n	69
大韓民國	Dàhán Míngwó Republic of Korea	n	73
大選	dàsywǎn general election	n	178
大陸	dàlù mainland, continent	n	24
大量	dàlyàng large quantity	n	162
大廈	dàsyà (or shà) mansion, big hall	n	71
大約	dàywē approximately	a	162

大衆	dàjùng masses, people	n	155
大綱	dàgāng an outline	n	143
大使	dàshř ambassador	n	39
大使館	dàshřgwǎn embassy	n	39
土耳其	Tǔěrchí Turkey	n	73
工業	gūngyè industry	n	95
工黨	Gūngdǎng Labor Party	n	179
廿	nyàn twenty	nu	110
上述	shàngshù above-mentioned	ph	210
上院	Shàngywàn House of Lords; Upper House	n	185
人士	rénshř persons (of distinction)	n	169
人口	rénkǒu population	n	15
人口調查登記	rénkǒu dyàuchá dēngji census	n	15
人員	rénywán personnel	n	122
人物	rénwù personage, a man of standing	n	85
川	chwān stream, riverlet	n	24
夕	syī (syì) evening (literary)	n	58
女性	nyǔsyìng female, women	n	28

4 Strokes

…方面	...fāngmyàn aspect, field, respect	n	179

予	yú give (lit.)	v	83
井	jǐng a well	n	160
王丙南	Wáng Bǐng-nán Wang Ping-nan	n	42
五彩	wǔtsǎi multicolor, colorful	n/sv	155
五月份	wǔywèfen the month of May	n	29
五強	Wǔ Chyáng Five Powers	n	180
夫人	fūrén Mrs., Madame, wife	n	40
支持	jīchí support	v/n	49
巴黎	Bālí Paris	pw	155
引用	yǐnyùng quote; cite	v	210
卅	sā (sà) thirty	nu	110
互助	hùjù mutual help	n	84
友邦	yǒubāng friendly nations	n	37
友好	yǒuhǎu friendship, goodwill	n	84
不斷	búdwàn continually, continuously	a	63
不但．．而且	búdàn...érchyè... not only...but also...	ph	87
不僅	bùjǐn not only	a	208
不僅．．而且	bùjǐn...érchyè... not only...but...	ph	87
戈	Gē (abbr. for *Gē'ěrbāchyáufū*)	n	201
戈爾巴喬夫	Gē'ěrbāchyáufū (Mikhail S.) Gorbachev	n	201

又	yòu still more, especially	a	155
以（N）	yǐ (N) with (N)	ph	125
以（V）	yǐ (V) so as to, to...(V)	cv-v	123
以期	yǐchī so as to (expect to)	ph	162
以及	yǐjí and	cv	24
以便	yǐbyàn so as to	ph	137
以…爲…	yǐ...wéi... to take...; to consider as	cv	15
以上	yǐshàng above..., more than	ph	29
以…而	yǐ... ér in order to... and	ph	187
日報	r̀bàu daily (newspaper)	n	6
日內	r̀nèi in a day or two	tw	162
日內瓦	Rnèiwǎ Geneva	pw	71
日程	r̀chéng program; schedule for the day	n	135
內閣	nèigé cabinet	n	177
內容	nèirúng contents	n	136
中東	Jūngdūng Middle East	pw	103
中華	Jūnghwá the Chinese (as a nation)	n	17
中華人民共和國	Jūnghwá Rénmín Gùnghégwó People's Republic of China	n	17
中華民國	Jūnghwámíngwó Republic of China	n	137
中南海	Jūng Nán Hǎi Chung Nan Hai Park	pw	50

中美	Jūng-Měi China and the United States	n	197
中美洲	Jūng-Měijōu Central America	n	203
中醫	Jūng-yī (abbr. for) Chinese medicine	n	197
中山公園	Jūngshān Gūngywǎn Sun Yat-sen Park	pw	51
中央	jūngyāng center/central	n/sv	111
中央(通訊)社	Jūngyāng (Tūngsyùn)Shè Central News Agency	n	6
中央政府	jūngyāng jèngfǔ central government	n	146
中國石油公司	Jūnggwó shŕyóu Gūngsž China Petroleum Company	n	161
比利時	Bǐlìshŕ Belgium	n	73
比合爾省	Bǐhé'ěr shěng Bihar state (India)	n	210
公司	gūngsž company, firm	n	161
公報	gūngbàu bulletin	n	17
公私合營	gūngsž héyíng managed jointly (public and private)	ph	95
公使	gūngshř minister (diplomacy)	n	39
公使館	gūngshřgwǎn legation	n	39
公佈	gūngbù make public	v	13
公約	gūngywē a mulitlateral treaty	n	84
月份	ywèfèn month	n	29
毛	máu hair/Mao (surname)	n	49
毛澤東	Máu Dzédūng Mao Tse-tung	n	50

升任	shēngrèn be promoted to...	v	94
及	jí and, together with	cv	24
今	jīn today (abbreviation)	tw	121
今晨	jīn chén this morning	tw	113
今午	jīn wǔ abbr. for jintyan jungwu	tw	121
分別	fēnbyé separately	a	147
仁	rén virtuous (lit.)	sv	190
反功	fǎngūng counter-attack	v/n	144
氏	shr̀ family name	n	201

5 Strokes

它	tā it (neutral gender)	pn	70
立院	Lìywàn abbr. of *lìfǎywàn*	n	146
立法院	Lìfǎywàn legislative Yuan	n	146
立即	lìjī (lìjí) at once, immediately	a	120
立場	lìchǎng position, standpoint	n	5
主席	jǔsyí chairman	n	49
主席台	jǔsyítái rostrum	n	49
主計長	jǔjìjǎng comptroller-general	n	146
市長	shr̀jǎng mayor	n	41

主要	jǔyàu major, essential	sv	61
主持	jǔchŕ take charge of	v	49
主人	jǔrén director	n	42
主體	jǔtí main issue	n	178
市場	shr̀chǎng market	n	170
示	shr̀ manifest, illustrate; order	v	83
平素	píngsù ordinarily	a	178
民族	míndzú nation, people	n	24
民國	míngwó a republic	n	73
未	wèi not (past), not yet (literary)	a	111
尼赫魯	Níhèlǔ Nehru	n	50
正式	jèngshr̀ formal/officially	sv/a	16
正當…的時候	jèngdāng...de shŕhoù when (or while) ...	ph	86
甘地	Gāndì Gandhi	n	52
甘廼迪	Gānnǎidí Kennedy	n	170
本	běn (one's) own, this	bf	125
本報	běn bàu this newspaper	n	125
本城	běn chéng this place/local	p	125
本週	běn jōu Honshu	pw	113
本人	běn rén one's self	pn	125

本月	běn ywè this month	tw	125
打鼓	dǎ gǔ drum	vo	049
打斷	dǎdwàn disrupt, interrupt	v	63
布爾加寧	Bùěrjyāníng Bulganin	n	61
布魯塞爾	Bùlǔsàiěr Brussels	pw	170
左右	dzwǒyòu approximately	n	113
皮杜爾	Pídùěr Bidault	n	72
召	jāu call, summon	v	70
召開	jāukāi to convene/convening	v/n	70
石油	shŕyóu petroleum	n	161
加深	jyāshēn deepen	v	161
加緊	jyājǐn speed up, intensify	v	161
加強	jyāchyáng strengthen	v	161
加速	jyāsù speed up, expedite	v	161
加大	jyādà enlarge	v	161
加入	jyārù join ; accede to (a treaty)	v	170
加入條約	jyārù tyáuywē accede to a treaty	vo	203
加拿大	Jyānádà Canada	n	73
目的	mùdì purpose	n	104
目前	mùchyán at present; now; presently	tw	198

另	lìng another; other; separate	p	211
另有打算	lìng yǒu dǎswàn have other plans	ph	211
另想辦法	lìng syǎng bànfa find some other way	ph	211
由	yóu by/from	cv	41
由	yóu from	cv	87
申	shēn notify, explain	bf	169
申請	shēnchǐng apply for	v	169
北京	Běijīng Beijing (Peking)	pw	17
北平	Běipíng Beijing (Peking)	pw	25
央	yāng the middle	bf	110
四川	Sżchwān Szechwan Province	pw	25
四國之行	sżgwó jř syíng a four-nation trip	ph	202
出產	chūchǎn produce	v/n	162
出租	chūdzū to let (for rent)	v	190
出路	chūlù way out; outlet	n	208
出席	chūsyí be present	v	049
台(臺)	tái terrace, platform	n	13
台灣	Táiwān Taiwan (Formosa)	pw	14
生效	shēngsyàu to become effective	vo	120
生活貧困	shēnghwó pínkwùn live in poverty	ph	211

印度	Yìndù India	n	50
白宮	Báigūng White House	n	184
付	fù hand over, pay, entrust	v	134
付諸實施	fù jū shŕshŕ put it into realization	ph	137
代表團	dàibyǎutwán delegation	n	59
仍	réng still	a	198
仍然	réngrán still; yet	a	198
奴	nú slave	n	102
奴隶	núlì slave	n	104
包括	bāukwò include	v	13
外交部長	wàijyāubùjǎng Minister of Foreign Affairs	n	85
外交部	wàijyāubù ministry of foreign affairs	n	41
外務相	wàiwùsyàng Foreign Minister	n	72
外僑	wàichyáu foreign nationals	n	14

6 Strokes

安全	ānchywán secure/safety, security	sv/n	103
安哥拉	Āngēlā Angola	n	203
次	tsż second, next	sv	191
次序	tszsyù (serial) order	n	69
次日	tszr̀ the next day	tw	191

次女	tsžnyǔ the second daughter	n	191
決議	jywéyì to resolve, decide	v	186
決議案	jywéyì'àn resolution (passed at a meeting)	n	186
宅	jǎi residence, dwelling	n	190
充實	chūngshŕ strengthen, to make full	v	186
亦	yì also (literary)	a	134
吉	jí auspicious, lucky (lit.)	sv	190
…地	...de adverbial ending	a	104
地方	dìfāng place/local	n/sv	95
地震	dìjèn earthquake	n/v	110
地區	dìchyū area, district	n	105
共	gùng (abbr.for *yígùng*) altogether	a	198
共黨	Gùngdang abbr. of *Gùngchǎndǎng*	n	146
共同	gùngtúng mutual, common	sv	121
共同市場	Gùngtúng Shr̀chǎng Common Market	n	170
共和國	gùnghégwó republic	n	17
西洋	syīyáng western hemisphere	n	156
西洋人	syīyángrén westerners	n	156
西班牙	Syībānyá Spain	n	198
西德	Syī-Dé West Germany	n	198

考慮	kǎolyù consider; think over	v	208
在…上	dzài...shàng on..., at...	ph	85
在…間	dzài...jyān between, among	ph	113
在…中	dzài...jūng in the midst/process of	ph	52
在…內	dzài...nèi in, within	ph	52
在…途中	dzài...tújūng on one's way to...	ph	137
在…後	dzài...hòu after...	ph	122
在…當中	dzài...dāngjūng among...	ph	198
在這方面	dzài jè fāngmyàn in this respect	ph	179
在飢餓之中	dzài jī'è jr̄ jūng in the (depths) of hunger	ph	211
有效	yǒusyàu effective	sv	120
有關	yǒugwān relate to/related/concerning	cv/bf	71
有利	yǒulì advantageous; favorable	sv	207
有利於	yǒulìyú be beneficial to	ph	207
存在	tswúndzài exist; be	v	211
再度	dzàidù once again	a	121
再三	dzàisān over and over again	a	202
再次	dzàitsż̀ once more; a second time	a	202
而	ér and, and yet,however, yet	cv/a	26
而且	érchyě moreover, furthermore	a	87

列	lyè arrange in order	v	144
列席	lyè syí attend a meeting without status	v	144
光華飯店	Gwānghwá Fàndyàn Kwanghwa Restaurant	n	191
早晨	dzǎuchén morning	tw	110
同情	túngchíng sympathy	n	87
同車	túngchē on the same vehicle	a	41
同機	túngjī on the same plane	a	40
同船	túngchwán on the same boat	a	41
同盟	túngméng alliance	n	82
同胞	túngbāu brethren, compatriot	n	144
曲	chyǔ ballads	n	155
因(因爲)	yīn (yīnwéi) because, on account of	bf	6
因此	yīn tsž therefore, because of this	ph	71
因素	yīnsù factor	n	178
因…之故	yīn...jrgù because of the reason	ph	171
回顧	hwéigù look back at; review	v/n	211
此	tsž this, here (lit.)	sp	71
此間	tsžjyān this place, here	pw	71
此地	tsždì this place	sp-n	71
此後	tsžhòu after this, hereafter	tw	71

艾登	Àidēng Eden	n	72
收復	shōufù to recover, take back	v	144
名	míng measure for persons	m	29
朱德	Jū Dé Chu Teh	n	60
年度	nyándù fiscal year, year	n	146
年齡	nyánlíng age	n	24
年限	nyánsyàn number of years (as a limit)	n	198
色彩	sètsǎi color, coloring, tinge	n	155
先後	syānhòu successively	ma	95
休會	syōuhwèi adjourn a meeting	vo	74
各界	gèjyè all walks of life	n	50
各自	gèdz each; repective; individual	p	202
仰光	yǎnggwāng Rangoon	pw	38
向	syàng to, toward	cv	63
任何	rènhé any (literary),	n	114
任命	rènmìng appoint/appointment	v/n	94
份	fèn portion, share	m	25
合作	hédzwò cooperate/cooperation	v/n	96
合作社	hédzwòshè cooperative stores	n	96
合眾國際社	Héjùng Gwójìshè United Press International	n	7

迅	syìn quick, hasty	sv/a	177
迅速	syìnsù prompt/speedily	sv/a	177
全體	chyáwntǐ whole, all the people	n	61
全體會議	chywántǐ hwèiyì plenary session	n	69
全國人民代表大會	chywángwó rénmíndàibyǎu dàhwèi National People's Congress	n	61
如此	rútsż as follows (lit.)	ph	135
如下	rúsyà as follows	ph	135
如上	rúshàng as above	ph	135
如後	rúhòu as follows	ph	135
好轉	hǎujwǎn improve	v	211
企	chǐ to look for	bf	102
企圖	chǐtú attempt	v	102
行	syíng travel; trip	n	202
行動	syíngdùng action, deed/ act; take action	n/v	104
行政院	syíngjèngywàn Executive Yuan	n	146

7 Strokes

況	kwàng condition	n	177
況且	kwàngchyě moreover	ma	177
沒有結束	méiyǒu jyéshù there is no end/endless	ph	201

社論	shèlwùn editorial	n	7
序	syù series, serial order	bf	69
牀(床)	chwáng bed	n	110
即(卽)	jí(jí) then, immediately; to be	a/v	120
即將	jíjyāng presently, very shortly	a	120
弄	nùng(lùng) small alley	n	191
形勢	syíngshr̀ situation; circumstances	n	208
形勢好轉	syíngshr̀ hǎujwǎn the situation improved	ph	211
局勢	jyúshr̀ situation, circumstances	n	86
改善	gǎishàn improve; improvement	v/n	210
抗	kàng oppose, resist	v	143
批	pī to comment upon/a batch	v/m	93
批評	pīpíng criticize/criticism	v	177
批準	pījwǔn ratify, approve/ ratification	v/n	94
批準書	pījwǔnshū instrument of ratification	n	121
攻	gūng attack	v	144
臣	chén officials	n	69
防御	fángyù defend/defense	v/n	120
杜勒斯	Dùlēsz̄ Dulles	n	72
李大章	Lǐ Dà-jāng Li Ta-chang	n	95

否	fǒu not, no (literary)	p/a	102
否認	fǒurèn deny	v	102
否則	fǒudzé otherwise (literary)	a	103
否決	fǒujywé veto	v	170
助理	jùlǐ assistant	n	42
見聞	jyànwén observation, experience	n	6
吳拉茂	Wú Lā Màu U La Maung	n	42
吳敏登	Wú Mǐn Dēng U Myint Thein	n	40
吳奴	Wú Nǔ U Nu	n	38
里斯本	Lǐszběn Lisbon	n	202
里根	Lǐgēn (Ronald) Reagan	n	201
男性	nánsyìng male, men	n	28
收獲	shōuhwò results; gains; (to) harvest	n/v	202
那拉底親王	Nàlādǐ Chīnwáng Prince Wan Waithayakon	n	73
妥	twǒ satisfactory, secure	sv	160
希臘	Syīlà Greece	n	73
邦	bāng state, country	n	37
私	sž private (versus public)	bf	5
私人	szrén private individual	n	5
利益	lìyì interest; benefit	n	208

我	wǒ our, us	p	38
住宅	jùjái residence	n	190
佈	bù spread, inform	v	13
佈告	bùgàu anounce/anouncement	v/n	13
作用	dzwòyùng function, effect	n	87
角度	jyǎudù angle; point of view	n	208
如果	rúgwǒ if	ma	6

8 Strokes

法	fǎ the law	n	40
法院	fǎywàn court	n	40
法官	fǎgwān judge	n	40
法新(社)	Fǎsyīn(shè) Agence France Presse	n	170
波特卡	Bwótèkǎ (place in Bihar state, India)	pw	210
河內	Hénèi Hanoi	pw	39
油井	yóujǐng oil well	n	160
油礦	yóukwàng oil deposits	n	160
定	dìng be scheduled	v	121
定	dìng settle, fix	v	82
定於	dìngyú be scheduled	v	121
定居	dìngjyū settle down; take up residence	v	211

官方	gwānfāng official circles	n	104
官邸	gwāndǐ official residence	n	134
並	bìng indeed	a	114
並	bìng moreover (abbr. for bìngchyě)	a	18
京戲	jīngsyì Peking opera	n	154
京劇	jīngjyù Peking (classical) opera	n	154
刻	kè at present	tw	137
於	yú at, in, to, than (literary)	cv	74
於…中	yú...jūng in the midst of	ph	113
於…起	yú...chǐ starting..., as of...	ph	122
性別	syìngbyé sex	n	26
表示	byǎushr̀ express; show; indicate	v	83
非洲之行	Fēijōu jr̄ syíng a trip to Africa	ph	202
武術	wǔshù martial arts	n	154
長	jǎng chief, head	n	41
長	jǎng to grow/senior	v/sv	191
長子	jǎngdž the eldest son	n	191
長女	jǎngnyǔ the eldest daughter	n	191
屆	jyè session, term (conference etc.)	m	154
屆時	jyèshŕ then, at that time	tw	192

居	jyū dwell, reside (literary)	v	110
居民	jyūmín inhabitants, residents	n	110
事宜	shìyí matters	n	135
事項	shìsyàng matters	n-m	71
東京	Dūngjīng Tokyo	pw	111
東南西北	dūng nán syī běi east, south, west, north	n	95
東西方關係	dūng-syīfāng gwānsyi East-West relations	n	203
亞	Yǎ Asia (abbr. of Yajou)	pw	70
亞洲	Yǎjōu Asia	pw	70
者	-jě one (that), those (who or which)	bf	4
其	chí his/her/their/its/that	pn	25
其實	chíshŕ as a matter of fact	ph	25
其余	chíyú the rest	sp	25
其中	chíjūng among (the preceding)	ph	198
其他	chítā other	sp	71
拒	jyù reject, refuse	v	169
拒絶	jyùjywé reject/refusal	v/n	169
招租	jāudzū to let (for rent)	v	190
招待	jāudài to entertain	v	84
招待會	jāudàihwèi a reception	n	84

擔	dān carry on pole, undertake	v	70
擔任	dānrèn undertake, take responsibility	v	70
抵	dǐ arrive at, reach (literary)	v	121
抵抗	dǐkàng resist/resistance	v/n	143
抵達	dǐdá arrive, reach	v	121
到達	dàudá arrive at	v	38
來賓	láibīn guest	n	58
來源	láiywán origin	n	160
杭州南路	Hángjōu Nán lù S. Hongchow Avenue	pw	191
阿比西尼亞	Ābǐsyīníyà Abyssinia	n	73
尚	shàng still, yet (literary)	a	170
明晨	míng chén tomorrow morning	tw	113
非洲	Fēijōu Africa	pw	70
咋舌	jà shé be flabbergasted	vo	156
呼籲	hūyù to appeal, plead	v	185
典禮	dyǎnlǐ ceremony, rite	n	61
具有	jyùyǒu have, possess	v	86
具有…意義	jyùyǒu...yìyì be of ... significance	vo	86
狀況	jwàngkwàng condition, circumstances	n	177
狀態	jwàngtài conditions, circumstances	n	184

周	jōu one turn or cycle/a surname	n	58
周恩來	Jōu En-lái Chow En-lai	n	52
周年	jōunyán anniversary	n	58
委	wěi commission, depute	v	59
委員	wěiywán a committee member	n	59
委員會	wěiywánhwèi committee, a commission	n	59
委員長	wěiywánjǎng committee chairman	n	59
的確	díchwè really, indeed	ma	24
制約	jr̀ywē restrict	v	207
制定	jr̀dìng work out; map out; formulate	v	208
爭取	jēngchyǔ strive for; stuggle for	v	208
延	yán delay, extend	v	155
延長	yáncháng extend, prolong/extension	v/n	155
物質	wùjr̀ material; matter	n	210
使	shř emissary, envoy	bf	39
使…得以	shř...déyǐ to enable (to cause...)	v	186
例如	lìrú for example	ie	6
佛教	fwójyàu Buddhism	n	210
近東	Jìndūng Near East	pw	103
返	fǎn return (literary)	v	134

邸	dǐ official residence	n	134
金礦	jīnkwàng gold mines	n	160
始	shř then, then only	a	179
往	wǎng go (literary)	v	39

9 Strokes

宣	sywān proclaim	bf	24
宣佈	sywānbù proclaim, announce	v	24
派遣	pàichyǎn send, dispatch	v	197
洲	jōu continent	n	70
美洲	Měijōu America	pw	70
美聯社	Měilyánshè Associated Press	n	6
美麗	měilì gorgeous, beautiful	sv	155
美術	měishù fine arts	n	154
前	chyán ex-, former	bf	40
前(任)	chyán(rèn) the former	sv	94
前夕	chyánsyī on the eve of	tw	58
前往	chyán wǎng go, leave for	v	39
前進	chyánjìn advance; forge ahead	v	208
前所未有	chyánswǒwèiyǒu unprecedented	ph	198
首	shǒu head, chief	n	38

首長	shǒujǎng chiefs, chief officials	n	126
首都	shǒudū capital (of a country)	n	38
首相	shǒusyàng prime minister	n	170
首領	shǒulǐng leader	n	82
首先	shǒusyān at first, first of all	a	86
首…及…	shǒu...jí at first... and subsequently	ph	147
客廳	kètīng parlor	n	38
帝	dì emperor	n	82
帝國	dìgwó empire	n	82
帝國主義	dìgwójǔyì imperialism	n	82
帝國主義者	dìgwójǔyìjě an imperialist	n	83
計劃	jìhwà plan	v/n	103
祝	jù wish, pray, praise	v	58
祝賀	jùhè congratulate	v	60
神聖	shénshèng sacred, holy	sv	145
實	shŕ carry out	bf	134
實行	shŕsyíng carry out, put into practice	v	134
施政	shŕjèng administration	vo	146
爲	wéi to be	v	25
爲	wéi; wèi by/be; for	cv/v	61

爲(了)	wèi(le) for the purpose of ...	cv	74
爲…計	wèi...jì for the purpose of... (lit.)	cv	161
爲…起見	wèi...chǐjyàn for the purpose of	cv	161
爲期	wéichī to last for; scheduled for	v/cv	202
飛抵	fēidǐ arrive by air	v	121
奏	dzòu play (musical instruments)	v	60
建國	jyàn gwó set up a nation	vo/n	60
按	àn (editor's) note	n	156
按照	ànjau according to, in accordance with	cv	120
城市	chéngshr̀ cities	n	26
城市建設總局	Chéngshr̀ Jyànshè Dzǔng Jyú General Board of Urban Redevelopment	n	96
赴	fù go (literary)	v	134
協	syé aid; harmonize	bf	169
協議	syéyì agreement, mutual consent	n	169
協助	syéjù aid	v/n	169
政務委員	jèngwù wěiywán member of the Executive Yuan	n	147
政黨	jèngdǎng political party	n	7
政策	jèngtsè policy	n	83
甚至於	shènjr̀yú even, to the point of	a	7
巷	syàng alley, lane	n	190

持	chŕ grasp, hold, support	v	49
持久	chŕjyǒu lasting; enduring; protracted	sv	208
指示	jřshr̀ order, instruct/instruction	v/n	83
指控	jřkùng accuse, denounce/charge	v/n	102
指出	jřchū point out	v	87
要題	yàutí main issue	n	178
括	kwò include	bf	13
括號	kwòhàu parentheses	n	14
威	wēi pomp, power	bf	102
威脅	wēisyé to threaten/menace	v/n	103
南日	Nánr̀ Nam Il	n	72
南還路	Nánhǎi Lù Nanhai Avenue	pw	191
南斯拉夫	Nánsžlāfū Yugoslavia	n	198
負	fù to bear on back	v	93
負責	fùdzé be responsible for	sv/vo	93
省長	shěngjǎng governor of a province	n	95
省份	shěngfèn province	n	29
咬	yǎu bite, gnaw	n	4
則	dzé then (as in “if...then”)	a	102
昨夜十時	dzwó yè shŕshŕ ten o’clock last night	tw	113

昨晚	dzwó wǎn yesterday evening or last night	tw	113
軍事	jyūnshr̀ military	sv	103
軍隊	jyūndwèi troops	n	60
軍械	jyūnsyè weapons of war	n	93
軍援	jyūnywán military aid	n	203
軍備	jyūnbèi armament	n	187
軍界	jyūnjyè the military	n	50
是否	shr̀fǒu is it or is it not, whether or not	av	102
界	jyè line of profession	bf	50
英迪拉甘地	Yīngdílā Gāndì Indira Gandhi	n	52
俞鴻鈞	Yú Húng-jyūn Yu Hung-chün	n	146
食物	shŕwù foodstuff; food;	n	211
胞	pāu womb, brethern	bf	144
香港	Syānggǎng Hongkong	pw	13
科	kē class or field; science	n	160
科學	kēsywé science	n	160
科學家	kēsywéjyā scientist	n	162
侵	chīn to invade, transgress	v	143
侵略	chīnlywè invade/ aggression	v/n	143
促	tsù to urge, press	v	177

後備兵	hòubèibīng reserve troops	n	186
後備兵法	Hòubèibīngfǎ Military Reserve Bill	n	186
保守	bǎushǒu conservative	sv	178
保守黨	Bǎushǒudǎng Conservative Party	n	178
保持	bǎuchŕ retain, keep	v	49
俄	È(É) Russia	n	145
約	ywē approximately	a	161
姚仲明	Yáu Jūng-míng Yao Chung-ming	n	40

10 Strokes

流亡	lyóuwáng go into exile	v	210
流亡政府	lyóuwáng jèngfǔ government-in-exile	n	210
海灣	hǎiwān gulf, bay	n	14
海峽	hǎisyá strait, (sea) channel	n	120
海外	hǎiwài overseas	n	18
海特	Hǎitè Hayter	n	85
消息	syāusyi news; tidings	n	197
準	jwǔn approve	v	93
宮	gūng palace	n	184
容	rúng accomodate	v	156
容納	rúngnà accomodate, take (in capacity)	v	156

兼	jyān and concurrently	cv	38
家	-jyā -ist	bf	162
宴	yàn banquet/to fete	n/v	49
案	àn a law-case, a proposal	n	93
討論	tǎolwùn discuss/discussion	v/n	74
記者	jìjě news reporter	n	4
記者招待會	jìjějāudàihwè press conference	n	136
記載	jìdzǎi record in history	v	13
訊	syìn(syùn) news, information	n	4
效	syàu efficacious, effectiveness	n/sv	120
效力	syàulì efficacy, effectiveness	n	120
被	bèi (a word indicating passive voice)	cv	111
袖	syòu sleeves	n	134
席	syí a mat, feast	n	49
座	dzwò seat/ measure for houses etc.	n/m	110
高文成	Gāu Wén-chéng (a ficticious name)	n	191
高等	gāuděng higher	sv	197
高等學校	gāuděng sywésyàu institution of higher learning	n	197
配	pèi to match	v	145
配合	pèihé to match, be coordinated	v	145

致	jr̀	v	70
	transmit, convey to		
致詞	jr̀ tsź	vo	82
	give a public speech		
致辭	jr̀ tsź	vo	70
	deliver a speech		
致電	jr̀ dyàn	vo	70
	send a telegram		
致賀	jr̀ hè	vo	70
	extend congratulations		
原油	ywányóu	n	162
	crude oil		
配備	pèibèi	v/n	162
	equip/equipment		
烈	lyè	bf	60
	ardent, fiery		
素	sù	n/s	178
	element/ordinarily		
泰國	Tàigwó	n	73
	Thailand		
馬尼拉	Mǎnílā	pw	125
	Manilla		
馬林科夫	Mǎlínkēfū	n	85
	Malenkov		
馬爾滕斯	Mǎertàisž	n	206
	(name of Prime Minister of Belgium)		
展延	jǎnyán	v	155
	extend		
原子	ywándž	n	187
	atom		
破裂	pwòlyè	v	169
	be broken, be broken down		
哥倫比亞	Gēlwúnbǐyà	n	73
	Columbia		
起程	chǐchéng	vo	37
	start on a journey		
起立	chǐlì	v	52
	stand up		
埃亞內斯	Aìyànèisž	n	203
	(name of President of Portugal)		

校長	syàujǎng president (of a college)	n	41
校友	syàuyǒu alumnus, alumna	n	192
校友會	syàuyǒuhwèi alumni association	n	192
校務	syàuwù school affairs	n	94
院	ywàn Yuan (see notes on p.148)	n	146
院長	ywànjǎng President of Yuan	n	146
院會	ywànhwèi Yuan meeting	n	146
孫明三	Swūn Míng-sān (a fictitious name)	n	191
根據	gēnjyù according to; in compliance with	cv	95
除…外	chú...wài besides, apart from	ph	113
除非…否則	chúfēi...fǒudzé unless...otherwise	ph	104
眠	myán sleep (literary)	n	111
財政部	Tsáijèngbù Ministry of Finance	n	146
財政部長	Tsáijèngbùjǎng Minister of Finance	n	146
茲	dž now, here, this (lit.)	tw	190
茲因	džyīn now because (of)	ph	190
峽	syá a gorge, strait	n	120
彩	tsǎi hue, color	n	155
氣象	chìsyàng climatic conditions	n	113
氣象台	chìsyàng tái observatory	n	113

秘	mì secret, private	bf	143
秘密	mìmì secret, confidential	sv	143
乘	chèng to ride, mount	cv	37
特此	tètsž (+ V) it is hereby ...	ph	192
租	dzū rent	v	190
紐約時報	Nyǒuywēshŕbàu The New York Times	n	15
紐約	Nyǒuywē New York	ow	15
留學	lyóusywé study overseas	v	197
留學生	lyóusywéshēng foreign (overseas) students	v	197
倫敦	Lwúndwūn London	pw	170
偕	syé accompany, together with	v/cv	58
偕同	syétúng accompany, together with	v/cv	58
條約	tyáuywē treaty	n	84
修正	syōujèng revise, correct/revision	v/n	186
修正案	syōujèngàn amendment	n	186
徐柏園	Syú Bwó-ywán Hsu Po-yüan	n	147
航	háng to sail/navigation (sea or air)	bf	93
航空	hángkūng navigate/navigation	v/n	93
航海	hánghǎi aviation	n	93
針灸	jēnjyǒu acupuncture and moxibustion	n	198

飢餓	jī'è hunger; starvation	n	211
般	bān sort, -way, -like	n	59
娛樂	yúlè amusement, entertainment	n	155

11 Strokes

淪	lwún be lost, degrade into	v	102
部	bù ministry, department	n	41
部長	bùjǎng minister (of a ministry)	n	41
部會	bùhwěi ministries and commissions	n	147
部署	bùshǔ deployment (military)	n	136
部長助理	bùjǎng jùlǐ assistant to the minister	n	42
部長會議	Bùjǎnghwèiyī Council of Ministers	n	85
商港	shānggǎng commercial port	n	13
訪	fǎng visit	v	37
訪問	fǎngwèn visit	v/n	37
訪友	fǎng yǒu call on a friend	vo	201
設立	shèlì set up/establishemnt	v/n	95
許多	syǔdwō many, a great many	nu	113
啓	chǐ open, begin	v	37
啓事	chǐshì a notice	n	191
啓程	chǐchéng start on a journey	vo	37

族	dzú race, clan	n	24
產量	chǎnlyàng output	n	162
登上	dēngshàng get onto	v	52
情勢	chíngshr̀ situation, trend of affairs	n	123
惟	wéi but, nevertheless	a	155
通過	tūnggwò pass (resolutions) through	v/cv	73
通訊	tūngsyìn communicate/communication	v/n	4
通訊處	tūngsyìnchù mailing address	n	4
通訊社	tūngsyùnshè news agency	n	4
現任	syànrèn the present	att	94
責	dzé responsibility	n	93
責任	dzérèn responsibility	n	93
規定	gwēidìng provisions; to stipulate	n/v	122
張霖之	Jāng Lín-jr̄ Chang Lin-chih	n	95
執	jŕ hold, manage	v	83
執行	jŕsyíng enforce, carry out	v	83
副	fù vice-, deputy	bf	59
副市長	fùshr̀jǎng deputy mayor	n	59
副主席	fùjǔsyí vice-chairman	n	59
專家	jwānjyā specialist, expert	n	162

專機	jwānjī special airplane	n	125
教育家	jyàuyùjyā educator	n	162
都妙意	Dū Myàu Yī Dau Mya Yee	n	40
黃國書	Hwáng Gwó-shū Huang Kuo-shu	n	147
基	jī base	bf	144
基地	jīdì basic	sv	144
基本	jīběn a base	n	144
基礎	jīchǔ foundation, basis	n	184
區	chyū region, area	n	110
械	syè implements	bf	93
麥克米倫	Màikèmīlwún Macmillan	n	170
莫桑比克	Mwòsāngbīkè Mozambique	n	203
梅蘭方	Méi Lán-fāng Mei Lan-fang (a famous actor)	n	156
控	kùng accuse, charge	v	102
控訴	kùngsù accuse/charge, a law suit	v/n	102
接着	jyēje subsequently	a	61
接受	jyēshòu accept	v	198
接受意見	jyēshòu yìjiàn take advice	vo	198
採油	tsǎi yóu drill (oil, etc.)	vo	161
採訪	tsǎifǎng cover; gather (news)	v	6

探	tàn search out, explore	v	160
探取	tànchyú explore/exploration	v/n	160
陸	lù land	n	24
陸地	lùdì dry land	n	24
陸軍	lùjyūn army, ground forces	n	24
達賴	Dá-lài Dalai (Lama)	n	210
張氏兄弟	Jāngshr̀ syūngdì The Jang brothers	n	201
逐	jú one by one (lit.)	bf	69
逐日	júr̀ day by day	ph	69
逐漸	jújyàn little by little, gradually	a	69
陪同	péitúng accompany	v	39
陶鑄	Táu Jù Tao Chu	n	94
盛	shèng abundant	sv	49
盛會	shènghwèi grand meeting/to hold a grand meeting	n/v	49
盛意	shèngyì generous intention	n	49
常委會	chángwěihwèi standing committee (abbr.)	n	94
常務委員會	chángwùwěiywánhwèi standing committee	n	59
略	lywè(lyàu) to seize, plunder; strategy	v/n	143
晨	chén morning	tw	110
莫洛托夫	Mwòlwòtwōfū Molotov	n	72

莊嚴	jwāngyán solemn	sv	61
荷蘭	Hélán the Netherlands (Holland)	n	73
將	jyāng (a word indicating the future)	a	74
國務	gwówù national affairs	n	94
國際	gwójì international	bf	145
國防	gwófáng National Defence	n	61
國防委員會	Gwófáng Wěiywánhwèi National Defence Council	n	61
國務院	Gwówùywàn State Council	n	61
國慶	gwóchìng National Day	n	58
國慶日	gwóchìngr̀ National Day	n	58
國慶節	gwóchìngjyé National Day	n	58
國會	Gwóhwèi Congress, Parliament	n	186
過據	gwójyù national opera (Peking opera)	n	154
國務卿	Gwówùchīng Secretary of State (U.S.)	n	69
國（際）聯（盟）	Gwó (jì) Lyán (méng) League of Nations	n	71
國家統計局	Gwójyā Tǔngjì Jyú State Statistic Board	n	15
國立西北大學	Gwólì Syīběi Dàsywé National Northwestern University	n	192
悉	syì know, understand (literary)	v	134
第三機械工業部	Dìsān Jīsyè Gūngyè Bù the Third Ministry of Machine Building	n	95
參院	Tsānywàn Senate	n	185

參議院	Tsānyìywàn Senate (U.S.)	n	185
參議員	Tsānyìywán Senator	n	185
頃	chǐng just now, a short while ago (lit.)	tw	184
俾	bì to enable, to the end that	v	145
假	jyǎ borrow, avail of	v	191
偵探	jēntàn spy	v/n	160
從事(於)	tsúngshr̀ (yú) be engaged in	v	162
從…獲悉	tsúng...hwòsyì it is learned from (lit.)	ph	197
術	shù a device, an artifice	n	155
途	tú way, road (literary)	n	134
貧困	pínkwùn poor; impoverished; poverty	sv/n	211

12 Strokes

渠	chyú he (literary)	pn	169
渠等	chyúděng they, them (lit.)	pn	184
測	tsè estimate, measure	v	160
測量	tsèlyáng measure, survey	v	160
測驗	tsèyàn test (academic)	n/v	160
港	gǎng port, harbor	n	13
港口	gǎngkǒu a port	n	13
勞工黨	Láugūngdǎng Labor Party	n	179

普選	pǔsywǎn general election	n	178
着重	jwójùng emphasize, stress	v	179
曾(曾)	tséng (a word indicating past)	a	110
曾經	tséngjīng already	a	211
詞	tsź word, phrase	n	82
評	píng criticize, discuss	v	177
評論	pínglwùn comment/commentary	v/n	177
就	jyòu with respect to, on	cv	103
就…是	jyòu...shr̀ with respect to the matter of ...	ph	137
登	dēng publish; ascend, mount	v	5
登報	dēngbàu publish in a newspaper	vo	5
登記	dēngjì register/registration	v/n	4
發源	fāywán originate	v	160
發表	fābyǎu make public, proclaim	v	103
發生	fāshēng occur, take place	v	111
報(紙)	bàu(jř) newspaper	n	6
報章	bàojāng newspaper	n	210
報道(報導)	bàudàu (bàudǎu) report	v/n	104
報館	bàugwǎn newspaper (office)	n	6
項	syàng for things or problems	m	71

彭真	Péng Jēn P'eng Chen	n	52
場	chǎng field, flat area	n	5
越南	Ywènán Vietnam	n	41
朝鮮	Cháusyan Korea	n	72
強大	chyángdà strong; powerful	sv	207
強調	chyángdyàu state emphatically	v	170
強烈	chyánglyè violent	sv	113
強制	chyángjr̀ compulsory	sv	186
強國	chyánggwó powers, powerful nations	n	179
隊	dwèi group, band	n	60
階	jyē steps (lit.)	n	145
階段	jyēdwàn phase, stage	n	145
階級	jyējí class (social), (military) rank	n	145
隆重	lúngjùng impressive (for ceremony, etc.)	sv/a	60
插曲	chāchyǔ episode	n	156
換文	hwànwén exchange of documents	vo	136
援	ywán help, assist	bf	84
援助	ywánjù aid, help	v/n	84
提出	tíchū put forward, submit	v	95
提供	tígùng provide; supply; furnish; offer	v	203

期間	chījyān during the period of...	tw	125
殖	jŕ(chŕ) plant, colonize	v	102
殖民地	jŕmíndì a colony	n	102
裂	lyè crack, split	v	169
賀	hè congratulate	v	60
掌	jǎng palm	n	49
最高人民撿察院	Dzwèigāu rénmín Jyǎnchyáwàn Supreme People's Procura-torate	n	61
晚	wǎn evening	tw	50
晚報	wǎnbàu evening paper	n	6
開採	kāitsǎi exploit, open (mines, etc.)	v	161
開幕	kāimù open (for conference, etc.)	vo	69
開會	kāihwèi hold a meeting	vo	51
開放	kāifàng open (to the outside / the public)	sv	207
開放政策	kāifàng jèngtsè (China's) "Open Door Policy"	n	207
間	jyān for rooms	m	191
貴賓	gwèibīn honorable guest	n	58
華	hwá abbr. for China	n	121
華南	Hwánán South China	pw	111
華北	Hwáběi North China	pw	111
華僑	hwáchyáu overseas Chinese	n	14

菲律賓	Fēilyùbīn the Philippines	n	73
菜市	tsàishr̀ vegetable market	n	191
等	děng and others, and other...	bf	40
策	tsè scheme, policy	bf	83
飯廳	fàntīng dining room	n	38
然後	ránhòu afterwards, then	ma	6
無家可歸	wú jyā kě gwēi homeless	ph	112
程	chéng journey, road	n	37
程序	chéngsyù sequence, order	n	70
進一步	jìn yībù further	a	105
集	jí assemble	v	102
集團	jítwán bloc	n	102
貿	màu trade	bf	169
貿易	màuyi trade	n	169
番	fān (for times, occasions)	m	202
粵	Ywè Kwangtung Province (Abbr.)	pw	93
衆(眾)	jùng a multitude, a crowd	n	155
衆院	jùngywàn House of Representatives	n	185
衆議員	Jùngyìywán Representatives	n	186
衆議院	Jùngyìywàn House of Representatives	n	185

堡壘廳	Băulĕitīng Fortress Hall	pw	122
順	shwùn follow, obey/convenient	v/sv	69
順利	shwùnlì smooth, smoothly	sv/a	69
順便	shwùnbyàn at one's convenience	n	69
卿	chīng high minister	n	69
統計	tŭngjì counting, statistics	n	15
統治	tŭngjr̀ to control; control/dominaiton	v/n	210
結束	jyéshù end; finish; conclude; close	n/v	201
結束講話	jyéshù jyănghwà wind up a speech	vo	201
給予	gĕiyù give	v	84
復	fù to repeat, recover, furthermore	v/a	144

13 Strokes

源	ywán source	n	160
滿意	mănyì satisfied; pleased; satisfaction	v/n	211
滇	Dyàn Yunnan Province (abbr.)	pw	111
滇西	Dyànsyī western Yunnan Province	pw	111
資本家	dzběnjyā capitalist	n	162
新西蘭	Syīnsyīlán New Zealand	n	73
新華社	Syīnhwáshè New China Agency	n	6
新任	syīnrèn the newly appointed	sv	94

意義	yìyì significance	n	86
廉	lyán reasonable in price/cheaply (lit.)	sv/a	190
詳盡	syángjìn exhaustive, detailed	sv	144
詢	syún(syùn) inquire	v	143
詢問	syúnwèn inquire, ask	v	143
電	dyàn cable, (telegraphic) dispatch	n	15
電機	dyànjī generator; electric motor	n	96
電力站部	Dyànlìjànbù Ministry of Power Stations	n	85
電台	dyàntái radio station	n	13
預算	yùswàn budget	n	146
瑞士	Rwèishr̀ Switzerland	n	74
瑞典	Rwèidyǎn Sweden	n	198
載	dzǎi record, carry	v	13
鼓	gǔ drum	n	49
鼓掌	gǔ jǎng clap the hands	vo	49
塔斯社	Tǎszshè Tass	n	7
搭機	dājī board an airplane	vo	136
損	swǔn damage, injure	v/n	111
損失	swǔnshr̄ to lose/loss	v/n	111
損害	swǔnhài damage	n	111

聖	shèng sacred, holy	sv	145
聖人	shèngrén a sage	n	145
聖經	shèngjīng the Bible	n	145
達	dá arrive at, reach	v	37
當前	dāngchyán the present, current	tw	123
當權	dāngchywán in power	vo	179
當政	dāngjèng in power	vo	179
署	shǔ a public office	n	185
署名	shǔ míng to sign (one's name)	vo	185
盟	méng an alliance/ to swear	bf	82
盟國	ménggwó allied states	n	82
盟邦	méngbāng allies, an allied nation	n	146
睡眠	shwèimyán sleep	n	111
照	jàu according to	cv	120
路透社	Lùtòushè Reuters	n	7
葉公超	Yè Gūng-chāu Yeh Kung-ch'ao	n	122
葡萄牙	Pútáuyá Portugal	n	202
敬悉…爲荷	jìngsyī...wéihé respectfully hope ...w/ appreciation	ph	192
業	yè already (literary)	a	135
業已	yèyǐ already	a	135

裝置	jwāngjr̀ install, set up	v	162
節目	jyémù program, repertoire	n	156
解救	jyějyòu free, rescue	v	147
解散	jyěsàn disperse, dissolve/dispersal	v/n	180
與	yǔ and, with (literary)	cv	120
毀	hwěi destroy, demolish	v	110
經	jīng through, after	cv	135
經營	jīngyíng manage	v	93
會	hwèi conference, meeting	n	51
會客	hwèikè meet with a guest	vo	201
會見	hwèijyàn meet with (esp. a foreign visitor)	v	201
會議	hwèiyì conference, meeting	n	69

14 Strokes

演	yǎn perform, drill	v	154
演習	yǎnsyí maneuver, drill (military)	n/v	186
演員	yǎnyuán actor, actress	n	154
演劇	yǎnjyù perform a play	vo	154
漢	Hàn Han Chinese	n	24
漢口街	Hànkǒu Jyē Hankou Street	pw	192
滲入	shènrù infiltrate	v	105

認爲	rènwéi be of opinion, hold (opinion)	v	180
賓	bīn guest	bf	58
賓客	bīnkè guest	n	58
精神領袖	jīngshén lǐngsyòu spiritual leader	n	210
慶賀	chìnghè congratulate	v	60
需	syū need	v	84
需要	syūyàu need	v/n	84
儘	jǐn to exhaust	v	144
劃	hwà plan	bf	103
赫魯曉夫	Hèlǔsyǎufū Khrushchev	n	60
歌唱	gēchàng singing	n	156
臺北市	Táipěishr̀ (city of) Taipeh	tw	122
惡	è (wù) evil, wicked	sv	177
惡感	ègǎn ill-feeling	n	177
惡化	è hwà to worsen	v	177
遠東	Ywǎndūng the Far East	pw	86
際	jí a border, limit	n	145
聞	wén it is learned (or heard) that	v	136
閣	gé cabinet (government)	n	177
數字	shùdż figure, number	n	15

數度	shùdù (for) several times	a	121
團	twán group	n	59
團長	twánjǎng head of a delegation	n	59
團員	twánywán member of a delegation	n	59
團體	twántǐ body, group	n	59
團結	twánjyé unite/unity	v/n	170
幕	mù curtain, screen	n	69
對抗	dwèikàng oppose, resist	v	143
對方	dwèifāng the other side	n	203
對…表示	dwèi...byǎushr̀ to express... concerning...	cv-v	86
對…來說	dwèi...láishwō as far as ... is concerned	ph	73
領	lǐng lead	v	82
領導	lǐngdǎu lead/guidance, leadership	v/n	82
領袖	lǐngsyòu leader	n	134
領導人	lǐngdǎurén leader	n	202
製	jr̀ make, manufacture	v	83
製造	jr̀dzàu manufacture	v	83
僑	chyáu lodge, sojourn	v	14
僑務	chyáuwù affairs of citizens overseas	n	94
僑民	chyáumín foreign nationals	n	14

種族	jǔngdzú race	n	24
稱	chēng say, state (lit.)	v	207
綱	gāng bond, principles	n	143
綱要	gāngyàu a summary	n	143
維	wéi maintain	v	83
維護	wéihù safeguard	v	83
維持	wéichŕ maintain, keep	v	83
態	tài manner, bearing	n	184
態度	tàidù attitude	n	184

15 Strokes

實施	shŕshr̄ carry out/implementation	v/n	134
適應	shr̀yìng to cope with, adapt/adjustment	v	123
談判	tánpàn negotiate/talks	v/n	170
談論	tánlwùn talk about; discuss	v	203
諸	jū (fusion of jr̄ yú)	ph	137
調	dyàu investigate	bf	13
調查	dyàuchá investigate/investigation	v/n	13
調任	dyàurèn be transferred (from a post to)	v	95
廣	gwǎng broad	sv	5
廣告	gwǎnggàu advertisement, notice	n	5

廣泛	gwǎngfàn broad (in nature)	sv	104
廣播	gwǎngbwō broadcast (radio)	v	13
廣東省	Gwǎngdūng Shěng Kwangdong Province	n	95
慶	chìng congratulate, celebrate	bf	58
慶祝	chìngjù congratulate, celebrate	v	58
震	jèn shock, shake	v	110
駐	jù to lodge, stationed at	b	37
駐蘇大使	jù Sū dàshř ambassador to the Soviet Union	n	84
熱烈	rèlyè warm, ardent	sv	60
熱心	rèsyīn ardent; enthusiastic	sv	208
撥	bwō to allot, transfer (as money)	v	190
撥冗	bwōrúng put one's multifarious affairs aside to	vo	192
輪	lwún revolve/ a wheel	v/n	70
輪流	lwúnlyóu in rotation/ to take turns	a/n	70
緊張	jǐnjāng tense	sv	86
播	bwō sow, disseminate	v	13
播音	bwōyīn broadcast	v	13
賴嘉文	Làijyāwén Raghaven	n	52
橫濱	Héngbīn Yokohama	pw	113
歐	Oū Europe	pw	83

歐洲	Oūjōu Europe	pw	83
歐洲共同體	Oūjōu Gùngtúng Tǐ The European (Economic) Community	n	203
歐美	Oū-Měi (Abbr.) Europe & (N.) America	n	197
確	chywè precise, reliable	sv/a	24
確實	chywèshŕ reliable, truthfully	sv/a	24
確數	chywèshù exact number	n	24
鄧小平	Dèng Syǎupíng Deng Xiaoping	n	207
選	sywǎn choose, select	v	197
選舉	sywǎnjyǔ vote, elect/election	v/n	178
暴	bàu violent, cruel	bf	59
暴風雨	bàufēngyǔ storm	n	59
劇	jyù theatrical plays; opera, drama	n	154
劇團	jyùtwán opera troup	n	154
劇院	jyùywàn opera house	n	154
餘	yú and plus, -odd	nu	15
舞	wǔ dance	v/n	155
舞蹈	wǔdǎu dance, folk dance	n	156
儀	yí ceremony	bf	121
儀式	yíshr̀ ceremony	n	121
劉少奇	Lyóu Shàu-chí Liu Shao-chi	n	61

劉曉	Lyóu Syǎu Liu Hsiao	n	84
億	yì 100,000,000	nu	13
僵	jyāng be stiff	sv	169
僵局	jyāngjyú deadlock	n	169
締	dì closely joined, a connection	bf	83
締結	dìjyé make (a treaty), form (an alliance)	v	83
編	byān edit	v	5
編排	byānpái edit/editing	v/n	5
編者	byānjě editor	n	5
緬甸	Myǎndyàn Burma	n	38
緩	hwǎn slow (lit.)	sv	178
緩和	hwǎnhé to ease	v	178
樂隊	ywèdwèi band (music)	n	60
質	jŕ(jr̀) to inquire/substance	v/n	143
質詢	jr̀syún inquire/questioning	v/n	143
徹	chè penetrate	v	60
徵	jēng to levy, recruit (troops), solicit	v	184
徵求	jēngchyóu to solicit, seek for	v	184
徵收	jēngshōu to levy and collect, as taxes	v	184
徵兵	jēng bīng to draft troops	vo	184

徵兵法	jēngbīngfǎ Draft Bill; Military Conscription Law	n	184

16 Strokes

澳大利亞	Àudàlìyà Australia	n	73
糖	táng sugar, candy	n	190
糖業	tángyè sugar industry	n	190
導	dǎu lead, guide	v	82
親王	chīnwáng prince	n	73
辦公廳	bàngūngtīng general office	n	38
謁	yè to visit (a superior)	v	134
諾	nwò answer, promise	v	178
諾言	nwòyán a promise, a pledge	n	178
聯席會議	lyánsyí hwèiyì joint meeting or session	n	122
聯合國	Lyánhégwó United Nations	n	104
聯邦	lyánbāng union, federation, federal	n/sv	37
機	jī airplane (abbr. of *fēijī*)	n	135
機場	jīchǎng airfield	n	135
機械	jīsyè mechanism, machinery	n	93
機器	jīchì machine, machinery	n	160
據	jyù according to	cv	50
據悉	jyùsyì it is known that	cv-v	134

據我所知	jyù wǒ suǒ jr̄ as far as I know	ph	197
據我看	jyù wǒ kàn as I see it; in my opinion	ph	197
檢	jyǎn examine	v	121
檢討	jyǎntǎu review and discuss	v	121
避	bì avoid	v	185
避免	bìmiǎn avoid	v	185
隨同	swéitúng accompany, follow	v	39
縣份	syànfèn county	n	29
器	chì tool, utensil	n	160
戰場	jànchǎng battlefield	n	104
戰略	jànlywè strategy	n	143
戰術	jànshù tactics	n	154
盧森堡	Lúsēnbǎu Luxembourg	n	73
暨	jì and, together with	cv	143
舉動	jyǔdùng act	n	103
舉行	jyǔsyíng hold (meeting)	v	51
學者	sywéjě scholar	n	4
學界	sywéjyè educational circles	n	50
學習	sywésyí study	n/v	197
學院	sywéywàn institute (educational)	n	197

17 Strokes

講話	jyǎnghwà give a talk (speech)	vo	60
講台	jyǎngtái speaker's platform	n	61
應	yìng respond, in respond to	cv	38
應邀	yìngyāu upon invitation	bo	39
應…需要	yìng...syūyàu to meet with the need of...	vo	161
營	yīng to manage (trade, etc.)	v	93
斃	bì kill, die a violent death	v	110
斃命	bìmìng be killed, be dead	v	110
聲明	shēngmíng announcement/announce	n/v	103
戴高樂	Dàigāulè De Gaulle	n	171
趨	chyū to hasten	v	177
趨勢	chyūshr̀ trend, tendency	n	177
擬	nǐ draft (a plan, etc.), intend	v	103
擬訂	nǐdìng draft	v	103
檢察長	jyǎnchájǎng procurator-general	n	61
戲	syì plays	n	154
戲劇	syìjyù theatrical plays, drama	n	154
雖…惟	swéi..., wéi although...yet	ph	156
獲	hwò acquire, obtain	v	59

獲致	hwòjr̀ attain, reach (an agreement)	v	170
獲得	hwòdé obtain, receive	v	59
邀	yāu invite	v	37
邀請	yāuchǐng invite/invitation	v/n	37
總	dzǔng general	bf	96
總預算案	dzǔngyùswànàn general budget bill	n	146
總局	dzǔngjyú general office	n	96
總司令	dzǔng sžlìng commander-in-chief	n	96
總理	dzǔnglǐ premier	n	38
總數(　字)	dzǔngshù(dž) total figure	n	15
總統	dzǔngtǔng president	n	6
御	yù to ward off, defend	v	120

18 Strokes and Over

灣	wān a bay, bend of a stream	n	14
謹	jǐn cautious, respectful/respectfully	sv/a	190
議	yì discuss	v	69
議案	yì'àn a proposal (on agenda)	n	93
議程	yìchéng agenda (of a meeting)	n	74
議決	yìjywé to resolve, to pass a resolution	v	186
議會	yìhwèi parliament; legislative assembly	n	203

讓	ràng cede, sell	v	191
讀者	dújě reader	n	4
顧	gù care for	v	169
顧問	gùwèn adviser	n	169
顧問委員會	gùwèn wěiywánhwèi advisory committee	n	207
競	jìng to strive, emulate	v	177
競爭	jìngjēng compete/competetion	v/n	177
競選	jìngsywǎn campaign (election)	v/n	177
龐松舟	Páng Sūng-jōu P'ang Sung-chou	n	147
廳	tīng hall	n	38
贏得	yíngdé win; gain; attain	v	207
懷仁堂	Hwáiréntáng Hall of Benvolence	pw	60
關於	gwānyú concerning	cv	17
麗	lì beautiful, elegant	sv	155
聽取	tīngchyǔ to hear, listen to	v	95
聽衆	tīngjùng audience	n	155
蠶桑	tsánsāng silkworm	n	198
擾	rǎu disturb, annoy	v/n	111
韓國	Hángwó Republic of Korea	n	73
礦	kwàng mines, mineral deposits	n	160

礦工	kwànggūng mine workers	n	160
礎	chǔ foundation, basis	bf	184
攜	syé (syī) carry, take with	v	169
嚴	yán stern, strict	sv	102
嚴重	yánjùng serious/gravely	sv/a	102
籲	yù to appeal	v	185
籲請	yùchǐng to plead	v	185
噸	dwūn a ton	m	160
藝	yì skill, craft, art	n	154
藝術	yìshù arts	n	154
觀衆	gwānjùng spectators, audience	n	155
觀禮	gwānlǐ watch the ceremony	vo	122
觀點	gwāndyǎn point of view	n	7
觀察	gwānchá observe/observation	v/n	180
觀察家	gwānchájyā observer	n	180
歡迎會	hwānyíng hwèi welcome party	n	51
蘇	Sū (surname)	n	5
蘇聯	Sūlyán Soviet Union	n	5
蘇俄	Sū'é Soviet Russia	n	145
蘇亞雷斯	Sūyàléisž (name of Prime Minister of Portugal)	n	203

驚恐	jīngkǔng consternation, panic	n	113
羅馬	Lwómǎ Rome	pw	170
羅素	Lwósù Russell	n	186
願	ywàn (abbr. for yuànyì) desire; want	v	201
齡	líng age	bf	24
覲謁	jìnyè to pay a visit to (chief of state)	v	136
辭	tsź words, expression	n	70
簽	chyān sign	v	82
簽字	chyāndż̀ sign name	vo	82
簽訂	chyāndìng sign, conclude (treaty,etc.)	v	82
簽名	chyānmíng sign name	vo	82
簽署	chyānshǔ to sign (one's name)	v	185
贊助	dzànjù support; assistance	n	207
雙方	shwāngfāng both sides, both parties	n	122
歸	gwēi return	v	110
歸國	gwēigwó return to (one's) country	vo	198
繼	jì succeed, continue, subsequently	v/a	144

APPENDIX A

30 Common Chinese Surnames
(approximate frequency order)

	W-G	(Yale)		W-G	(Yale)
王	Wang	(Wáng)	宋	Sung	(Sùng)
李	Li	(Lǐ)	胡	Hu	(Hú)
張	Chang	(Jāng)	何	Ho	(Hé)
趙	Chao	(Jàu)	錢	Ch'ien	(Chyán)
劉	Liu	(Lyóu)	林	Lin	(Lín)
陳	Ch'en	(Chén)	許	Hsü	(Syǔ)
高	Kao	(Gāu)	鄭	Cheng	(Jèng)
楊	Yang	(Yáng)	沈	Shen	(Shěn)
吳	Wu	(Wú)	蔣	Chiang	(Jyǎng)
周	Chou	(Jōu)	曹	Ts'ao	(Tsáu)
黃	Huang	(Hwáng)	葉	Yeh	(Yè)
徐	Hsü	(Syú)	郭	Kuo	(Gwō)
朱	Chu	(Jū)	孫	Sun	(Swūn)
馬	Ma	(Mǎ)	程	Ch'eng	(Chéng)
韓	Han	(Hán)	梁	Liang	(Lyáng)

The above is only a partial list. The student should note that romanized spelling of Chinese surnames varies considerably. Many deviations will be encountered with the Wade-Giles spellings predominating. *Pin-yin* spellings are now also seen increasingly since China adopted the *pin-yin* romanization.

APPENDIX B

Chinese Transliteration

Following are some of the general rules observed in transliteration of foreign names into Chinese:

1. Each syllable in a foreign name is represented by a similar Chinese sound, while consonant clusters are usually broken down and represented each with a similar Chinese sound. For example:

Clark 克拉克　　Jordan 約但

Istanbul 伊士丹步爾　　Eisenhower 艾森豪威爾

Scandinavia 斯堪地那維亞

2. The Chinese Characters to represent these sounds are usually those which do not appear in daily speech usage and many have very remote or no meaning. For example:

Hull 赫爾　　Manchester 曼徹斯特

Washington 華盛頓　　Alaska 阿拉斯加

Abyssinia 阿比西尼亞

3. Some common daily used characters are used but their meanings are so far removed from the news items that the reader can judge that it is their sound and not their meaning that is to be considered. And because of this, a combination of rare-meaning and commonly used characters often indicate a foreign name. For example:

Canada 加拿大　　Geneva 日內瓦

Columbia 哥倫比亞　　Cairo 開羅

Turkey 土耳其

4. With names of people, the tendency is to transliterate them into 2 or 3 characters and if possible match the first or initial syllable with

Chinese characters that are Chinese surnames. These surnames usually have no meaning. For examples:

Trumen	杜魯門	Wagner	韋格納
Churchill	邱吉爾	Anderson	安德生
Pandit	潘迪特		

5. Names of people are often abbreviated by keeping the surname and adding the word 氏 (shr̀) or the official title behind it. These abbreviations often appear after the full names have been mentioned. For example:

		abbreviated:
Dulles	杜勒斯	杜氏
Truman	杜魯門	杜總統

6. Parts in foreign place names are often translated by their meanings into Chinese characters such as:

New....	is translated into	新
West....	"	西
St.	"	聖
....burg	"	堡

For example:

New Delhi	新德里	St. Louis	聖路易
New Zealand	新西蘭	St. Petersburg	聖彼得堡
West Germany	西德	Luxemburg	盧森堡

7. Names of states in the U.S. and well-known cities are often abbreviated by keeping the first syllable and attaching 省 (state), or 城 (city) behind. For example:

麻 省 (Má shěng) for Massachusetts

費 城 (Fèi chéng) for Philadelphia

支(芝)城 (Jr̄ chéng) for Chicago

8. Names of countries are often abbreviated by keeping the first character. For example:

英 for England 英格蘭　　法 for France 法蘭西

德 for Germany 德意志　　印 for India 印度

9. In transliteration 'r' and 'l' are often not distinguished. When a syllable ends in 'l', the 'l' is often transliterated by "er" sound as

Churchill 邱吉爾　　Nepal 尼泊爾

Marshall 馬歇爾

10. When a syllable begins with 'r', the 'r' is often transliterated by 'l' sound as

Rumania 羅馬尼亞　　Peru 秘魯

Robertson 羅泊生　　Syria 叙利亞

Cairo 開羅　　Paraguay 巴拉圭

11. Differenciation between P B, T D and K G are often not made. For example:

Panama 巴拿馬　　Cuba 古巴

Paris 巴黎　　Batavia 巴達維亞

Washington 華盛頓　　Tito 狄托

Martin 馬丁　　Van Fleet 萬福利得

Columbia 哥侖比亞	Cleveland 克利夫蘭
Chicago 芝加哥	Gottwald 高德華

APPENDIX C

PEOPLE'S REPUBLIC OF CHINA

Organization of the Central Government

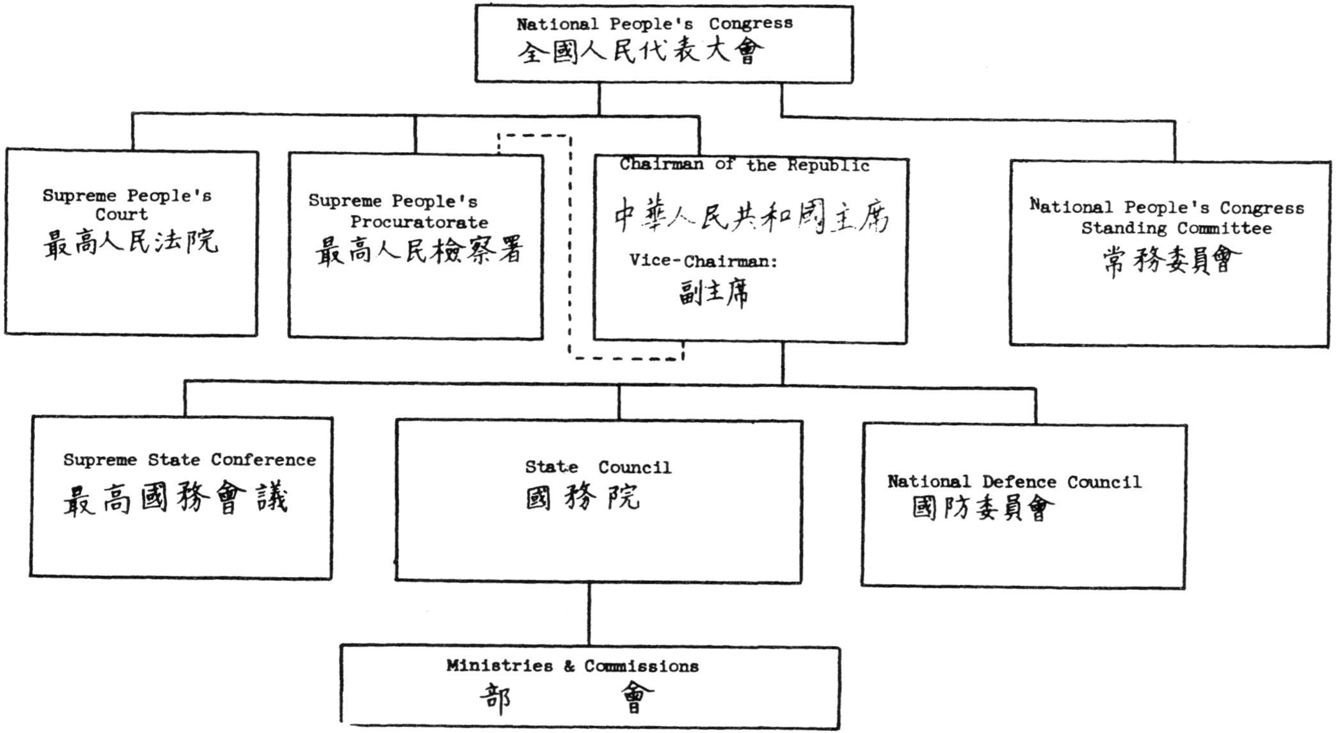

APPENDIX D

ORGANIZATION OF THE CENTRAL GOVERNMENT

THE REPUBLIC OF CHINA

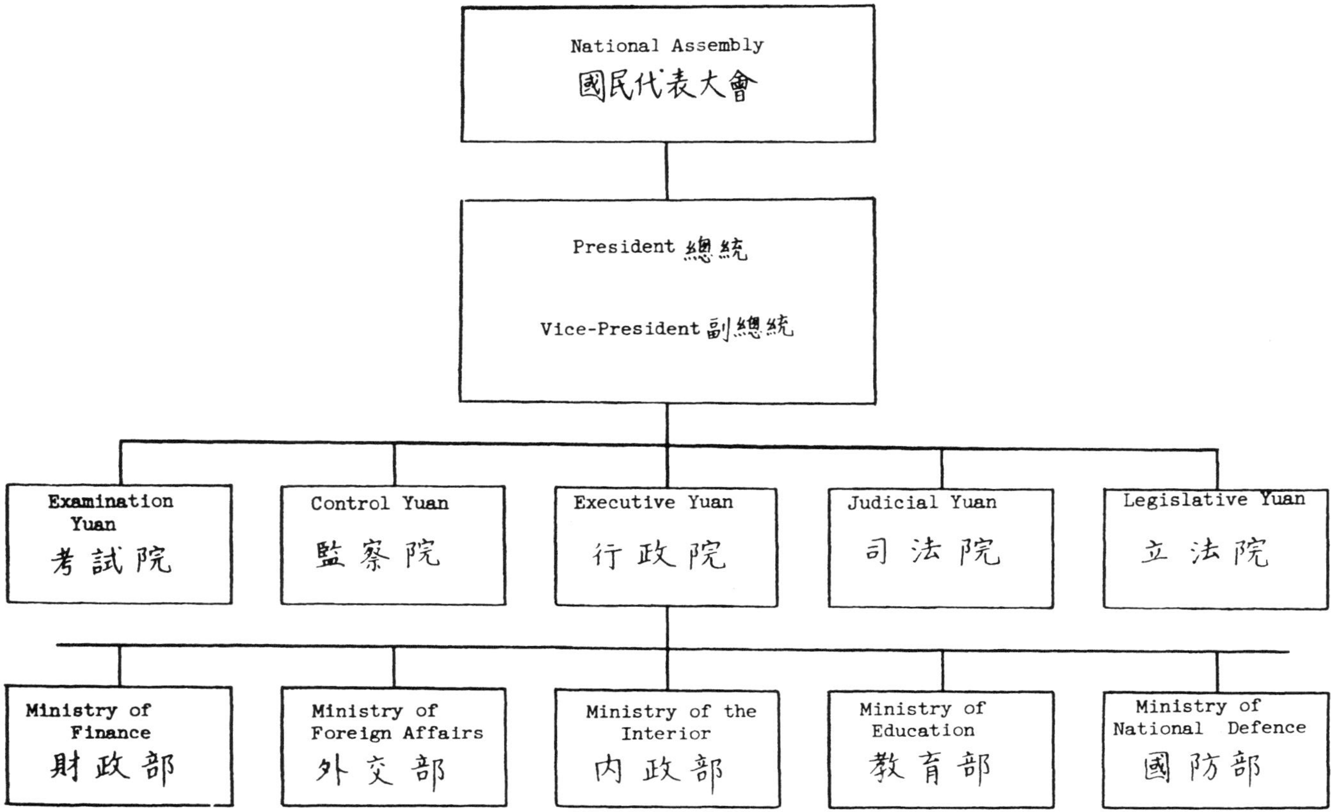

APPENDIX E

Literary-Vernacular Comparative Lists

The following are three lists of literary words together with their vernacular counterparts. The great majority of the words have appeared in this book; those not appearing in the book are given their pronunciations.

I. Nouns, Pronouns, Specifiers

Literary	Vernacular	English Meaning
吾(wú), 予 (yú), 余(yu)	我	I, me
我人,我等,吾人	我們	we, us
汝 (rǔ)	你	you
汝等	你們	you
彼,渠,	他	he, him
彼等,渠等	他們	they, them
此,本,斯 (sz̄)	這個	this
彼,其	那個	that
何	甚麼	what?
者	的人,的東西	one that
之	它,它們	it, them

II. Verbs, Coverbs

Literary	Vernacular	English Meaning
為,係,即,乃 (nǎi)	是	to be
謂,稱,宣稱,聲稱,云	說	say, state
與,及,以及,暨	跟,和,同	and, with
無	沒有	have no
抵,達,至	到	arrive at
赴,往	去	go
返	回	return
似,如,若	像,好像	resemble, be like
自,由	從,自從	from
於	在	at, in, than, etc

III. Adverbs, Connectives, Particles

Literary	Vernacular	English Meaning
甚,至,殊 (shū)	很	very
頗	很,相當	quite
皆,均	都	all
未	没,(没有)	not
亦	也	also
則	就	then
即,立即	就,立刻	instantly
惟,然,然而	可是,但,但是	but, however
故	所以	therefore
如何	怎麼	how?
尚	還	yet, still
始	才	then only, until
如	如果,要是	if
之	的,底	of
復	又	again, once more

APPENDIX F: 800 Basic Characters

Here is a list of 800 characters, recognition of which is assumed as a prerequisite to the use of this text. It contains the 300 in Read Chinese, the 300 in Read About China, and another 200 chosen at the author's discretion. The characters are arranged in the numerical order of their radicals.

1 (一) 一 七 上 下 三 不 且 世 丟 並

2 (丨) 中

3 (丶) 主

4 (丿) 久 之

5 (乙) 九 也 乾 亂

6 (亅) 了 事

7 (二) 二 互 五 些

8 (亠) 交 京 亮

9 (人) 人 今 介 仍 他 代 令 以 件 任 休 你 但 位 低 住 何 作 佔 使 來 例 便 俗 保 信 修 個 們 倒 候 借 倍 值 假 停 偷 備 傳 傷 像 價

10 (儿) 元 兄 先 光 免 兒

11 (入) 入 內 全 兩

12 (八) 八 公 六 共 兵 其 典 具

13 (冂) 再

15 (冫) 冬 決 冷

16 (几) 凡

17 (凵) 出

18 (刀) 刀 分 切 初 別 利 到

制刻前剛創

19
(力)
力功加助努動務勝勞勢勸

20
(勹)
包

21
(匕)
化北

24
(十)
十千午升半南

26
(卩)
危印

27
(厂)
厚原

28
(厶)
去參

29
(又)
又友反取受

30
(口)
口古句只可叫史右司另吃各合同名向吸吹告吧呢味命和品員哥哭唱商問喝喜單嗎

31
(囗)
四回因困國圍園圓圖

32
(土)
土在地坐城堂報塊壞

33
(士)
士

34
(夊)
夏

36
(夕)
外多夜夠

37
(大)
大天太夫失奇

38
(女)
女好如妹妻始姐姓婦婚

39
(子)
子字存孩孫學

40
(宀)
守安完宗官定宜客室害家容寄密富實寫寬寶

41
(寸)
寸封將專對

42

〔小〕 小 少

43 〔尢〕 就

44 〔尸〕 尺 局 屋 展 屬

46 〔山〕 山

48 〔工〕 工 左 差

49 〔己〕 己 已

50 〔巾〕 市 布 希 師 帶 常 帽 幫

51 〔干〕 平 年 幸

52 〔幺〕 幾

53 〔广〕 底 店 府 度

54 〔廴〕 建

55 〔廾〕 弄

56 〔弋〕 式

57 〔弓〕 弟 張 強

59 〔彡〕 形 影

60 〔彳〕 彼 往 待 很 後 得 從

61 〔心〕 心 必 忘 忙 快 念 忽 怎 怒 怕 思 急 性 怪 恐 恥 息 您 情 惜 惡 想 愈 愁 意 愛 慢 憐 懂 應

62 〔戈〕 成 我 或 戰

63 〔戶〕 房 所

64 〔手〕 手 才 打 找 把 抱 拉 招 拜 指 按 拿 捉 掉 掃 掛 接 推 提 換 據

65 〔支〕 支

66 〔攴〕 收 改 放 政 故 教 救 敗 敢 散 敬 數 整

67 〔文〕 文

68 〔斗〕 料

69 〔斤〕 斤 新 斷

70 〔方〕 方 於 旁

旅旗

71
〔无〕既

72
〔日〕日早明易星春昨是時晚普景暗暫

73
〔曰〕更書最替會

74
〔月〕月有朋服望期

75
〔木〕木本村李東板林果查校根桌條極楚業概樂樓樣樹橋機模

76
〔欠〕次歌歡

77
〔止〕止正此步歲歷

78
〔歹〕死

79
〔殳〕段殺

80
〔毋〕母每

81
〔比〕比

82
〔毛〕毛

83
〔氏〕民

84
〔气〕氣

85
〔水〕水永求江沒汽沙河油治法注洋洗洞活派流海消涼淡淨深清淺減湖溫準滿漸

86
〔火〕火災無然煙照熱燈燒

87
〔爪〕爭爲

88
〔父〕父

90
〔爿〕牆

91
〔片〕片

93
〔牛〕牛物特

94
〔犬〕狀狗

96
〔玉〕玉王玩現球理

97
〔瓜〕瓜

99
〔甘〕
甚
100
〔生〕
生產
101
〔用〕
用
102
〔田〕
田由男界
留畫當
104
〔疒〕
病痛
105
〔癶〕
發
106
〔白〕
白百的
107
〔皮〕
皮
109
〔目〕
目直着相省看眞眼睡
111
〔矢〕
知短
112
〔石〕
石破研
113
〔示〕
社祖神票禁福禮
115
〔禾〕
私秋
程種稱
116
〔穴〕
究空穿窗窮
117
〔立〕
立站
118
〔竹〕
竹
笑第筆等答算管節範簡
119
〔米〕
米粉精
120
〔糸〕
紀
約紅紙級細組紹結給統絲經緊線縣總織
121
〔缶〕
缺
123
〔羊〕
羊美羣義
124
〔羽〕
習
125
〔老〕
老考
126
〔而〕
而
128
〔耳〕
耳聞聯聰聲職聽
130
〔肉〕
肉肯背能脫脚
臉
132
〔自〕
自
134
〔臼〕
興舉舊
137
〔舟〕
船
139
〔色〕
色

140 (艸)
花若苦英茶草菜華萬落葉薄藏藥

141 (虍)
處號

143 (血)
血

144 (行)
行街

145 (衣)
衣表被裏補裝複

146 (襾)
西要

147 (見)
見規親覺觀

148 (角)
角解

149 (言)
計討記設許訴試話該詳認語說誰課談請論講謝證識讀護變讓

154 (貝)
財貨貴買費賣賊

156 (走)
走起越趕趣

157 (足)
足跑路跟跳

158 (身)
身

159 (車)
車軍較輕轉

160 (辛)
辦

161 (辰)
農

162 (辵)
近迎迷追退送逃這通速造連進遇遊運過道遠適選還邊

163 (邑)
那部都郵鄉鄰

164 (酉)
酒醒醫

166 (里)
里重野量

167 (金)
金銀銅鋪錢錯鐘鐵

168 (長)
長

169 (門)
門

閑 開 間 關 170 〔阜〕 防 限 院 除 降 陰 陽 隨 險 172 〔隹〕 隻

雖 雙 雜 離 難 173 〔雨〕 雨 雲 零 電 露 174 〔青〕 青 靜 175

〔非〕 非 靠 176 〔面〕 面 177 〔革〕 革 180 〔音〕 音 響 181 〔頁〕 頂

須 預 頭 題 願 類 顯 182 〔風〕 風 183 〔飛〕 飛 184 〔食〕 食 飯

養 餘 館 186 〔香〕 香 187 〔馬〕 馬 驗 驚 188 〔骨〕 體 189 〔高〕

高 191 〔鬥〕 鬧 195 〔魚〕 魚 196 〔鳥〕 鳥 200 〔麻〕 麼 201 〔黃〕

黃 203 〔黑〕 黑 點 黨 210 〔齊〕 齊

COMPARATIVE TRANSCRIPTION TABLE

Yale Wade-Giles Pinyin

Yale	Wade-Giles	Pinyin
a	a	a
ai	ai	ai
an	an	an
ang	ang	ang
au	ao	ao
ba	pa	ba
bai	pai	bai
ban	pan	ban
bang	pang	bang
bau	pao	bao
bei	pei	bei
ben	pen	ben
beng	peng	beng
bi	pi	bi
bin	pin	bin
bing	ping	bing
bou	pou	bou
bu	pu	bu
bwo	po	bo
byan	pien	bian
byau	piao	biao
bye	pieh	bie
cha	ch'a	cha
chai	ch'ai	chai
chan	ch'an	chan
chang	ch'ang	chang
chau	ch'ao	chao
che	ch'e	che
chen	ch'en	chen
cheng	ch'eng	cheng
chi	ch'i	qi
chin	ch'in	qin
ching	ch'ing	qing
chou	ch'ou	chou
chr	ch'ih	chi
chu	ch'u	chu
chung	ch'ung	chong
chwai	ch'uai	chuai
chwan	ch'uan	chuan
chwang	ch'uang	chuang
chwei	ch'ui	chui
chwo	ch'o	chuo
chwun	ch'un	chun
chya	ch'ia	qia
chyan	ch'ien	qian
chyang	ch'iang	qiang
chyau	ch'iao	qiao
chye	ch'ieh	qie
chyou	ch'iu	qiu
chyu	ch'ü	qu
chyun	ch'ün	qun
chyung	ch'iung	qiong
chywan	ch'üan	quan
chywe	ch'üeh	que
da	ta	da
dai	tai	dai
dan	tan	dan
dang	tang	dang
dau	tao	dao
de	te	de
dei	tei	dei
deng	teng	deng
di	ti	di
ding	ting	ding
dou	tou	dou
du	tu	du
dung	tung	dong
dwan	tuan	duan
dwei	tui	dui
dwo	to	duo
dwun	tun	dun
dyan	tien	dian
dyau	tiao	diao
dye	tieh	die
dyou	tiu	diu
dz	tzu	zi
dza	tsa	za
dzai	tsai	zai
dzan	tsan	zan
dzang	tsang	zang
dzau	tsao	zao
dze	tse	ze
dzei	tsei	zei
dzen	tsen	zen
dzeng	tseng	zeng
dzou	tsou	zou
dzu	tsu	zu
dzung	tsung	zong
dzwan	tsuan	zuan
dzwei	tsui	zui
dzwo	tso	zuo
dzwun	tsun	zun
e	e, o	e
ei	ei	ei

Yale	Wade-Giles	Pinyin
en	en	en
eng	eng	eng
er	erh	er
fa	fa	fa
fan	fan	fan
fang	fang	fang
fei	fei	fei
fen	fen	fen
feng	feng	feng
fou	fou	fou
fu	fu	fu
fwo	fo	fo
ga	ka	ga
gai	kai	gai
gan	kan	gan
gang	kang	gang
gau	kao	gao
ge	ke, ko	ge
gei	kei	gei
gen	ken	gen
geng	keng	geng
gou	kou	gou
gu	ku	gu
gung	kung	gong
gwa	kua	gua
gwai	kuai	guai
gwan	kuan	guan
gwang	kuang	guang
gwei	kuei	gui
gwo	kuo	guo
gwun	kun	gun
ha	ha	ha
hai	hai	hai
han	han	han
hang	hang	hang
hau	hao	hao
he	ho	he
hei	hei	hei
hen	hen	hen
heng	heng	heng
hou	hou	hou
hu	hu	hu
hung	hung	hong
hwa	hua	hua
hwai	huai	huai
hwan	huan	huan
hwang	huang	huang
hwei	hui	hui
hwo	huo	huo
hwun	hun	hun
ja	cha	zha
jai	chai	zhai
jan	chan	zhan
jang	chang	zhang
jau	chao	zhao
je	che	zhe
jei	chei	zhei
jen	chen	zhen
jeng	cheng	zheng
ji	chi	ji
jin	chin	jin
jing	ching	jing
jou	chou	zhou
jr	chih	zhi
ju	chu	zhu
jung	chung	zhong
jwa	chua	zhua
jwai	chuai	zhuai
jwan	chuan	zhuan
jwang	chuang	zhuang
jwei	chui	zhui
jwo	cho	zhuo
jwun	chun	zhun
jya	chia	jia
jyan	chien	jian
jyang	chiang	jiang
jyau	chiao	jiao
jye	chieh	jie
jyou	chiu	jiu
jyu	chü	ju
jyun	chün	jun
jyung	chiung	jiong
jywan	chüan	juan
jywe	chüeh	jue
ka	k'a	ka
kai	k'ai	kai
kan	k'an	kan
kang	k'ang	kang
kau	k'ao	kao
ke	k'e, k'o	ke
ken	k'en	ken
keng	k'eng	keng
kou	k'ou	kou
ku	k'u	ku
kung	k'ung	kong
kwa	k'ua	kua
kwai	k'uai	kuai
kwan	k'uan	kuan
kwang	k'uang	kuang
kwei	k'uei	kui
kwo	k'uo	kuo
kwun	k'un	kun
la	la	la
lai	lai	lai
lan	lan	lan
lang	lang	lang
lau	lao	lao
le	le	le
lei	lei	lei
leng	leng	leng

Yale	Wade-Giles	Pinyin	Yale	Wade-Giles	Pinyin
li	li	li	nyau	niao	niao
lin	lin	lin	nye	nieh	nie
ling	ling	ling	nyou	niu	niu
lou	lou	lou	nyu	nü	nü
lu	lu	lu	nywe	nüeh	nüe
lung	lung	long			
lwan	luan	luan	ou	ou	ou
lwo	lo	luo			
lwun	lun	lun	pa	p'a	pa
lya	lia	lia	pai	p'ai	pai
lyan	lien	lian	pan	p'an	pan
lyang	liang	liang	pang	p'ang	pang
lyau	liao	liao	pau	p'ao	pao
lye	lieh	lie	pei	p'ei	pei
lyou	liu	liu	pen	p'en	pen
lyu	lü	lü	peng	p'eng	peng
lywan	lüan	lüan	pi	p'i	pi
lywe	lüeh	lüe	pin	p'in	pin
			ping	p'ing	ping
ma	ma	ma	pou	p'ou	pou
mai	mai	mai	pu	p'u	pu
man	man	man	pwo	p'o	po
mang	mang	mang	pyan	p'ien	pian
mau	mao	mao	pyau	p'iao	piao
mei	mei	mei	pye	p'ieh	pie
men	men	men			
meng	meng	meng	r	jih	ri
mi	mi	mi	ran	jan	ran
min	min	min	rang	jang	rang
ming	ming	ming	rau	jao	rao
mou	mou	mou	re	je	re
mu	mu	mu	ren	jen	ren
mwo	mo	mo	reng	jeng	reng
myan	mien	mian	rou	jou	rou
myau	miao	miao	ru	ju	ru
mye	mieh	mie	rung	jung	rong
myou	miu	miu	rwan	juan	ruan
			rwei	jui	rui
na	na	na	rwo	jo	ruo
nai	nai	nai	rwun	jun	run
nan	nan	nan			
nang	nang	nang	sa	sa	sa
nau	nao	nao	sai	sai	sai
ne	ne	ne	san	san	san
nei	nei	nei	sang	sang	sang
nen	nen	nen	sau	sao	sao
neng	neng	neng	se	se	se
ni	ni	ni	sen	sen	sen
nin	nin	nin	seng	seng	seng
ning	ning	ning	sha	sha	sha
nou	nou	nou	shai	shai	shai
nu	nu	nu	shan	shan	shan
nung	nung	nong	shang	shang	shang
nwan	nuan	nuan	shau	shao	shao
nwo	no	nuo	she	she	she
nwun	nun	nun	shei	shei	shei
nyan	nien	nian	shen	shen	shen
nyang	niang	niang	sheng	sheng	sheng

Yale	Wade-Giles	Pinyin	Yale	Wade-Giles	Pinyin
shou	shou	shou	tsau	ts'ao	cao
shr	shih	shi	tse	ts'e	ce
shu	shu	shu	tsen	ts'en	cen
shwa	shua	shua	tseng	ts'eng	ceng
shwai	shuai	shuai	tsou	ts'ou	cou
shwan	shuan	shuan	tsu	ts'u	cu
shwang	shuang	shuang	tsung	ts'ung	cong
shwei	shui	shui	tswan	ts'uan	cuan
shwo	shuo	shuo	tswei	ts'ui	cui
shwun	shun	shun	tswo	ts'o	cuo
sou	sou	sou	tswun	ts'un	cun
su	su	su	tsz	tz'u	ci
sung	sung	song	tu	t'u	tu
swan	suan	suan	tung	t'ung	tong
swei	sui	sui	twan	t'uan	tuan
swo	so	suo	twei	t'ui	tui
swun	sun	sun	two	t'o	tuo
sya	hsia	xia	twun	t'un	tun
syan	hsien	xian	tyan	t'ien	tian
syang	hsiang	xiang	tyau	t'iao	tiao
syau	hsiao	xiao	tye	t'ieh	tie
sye	hsieh	xie			
syi	hsi	xi	wa	wa	wa
syin	hsin	xin	wai	wai	wai
sying	hsing	xing	wan	wan	wan
syou	hsiu	xiu	wang	wang	wang
syu	hsü	xu	wei	wei	wei
syun	hsün	xun	wen	wen	wen
syung	hsiung	xiong	weng	weng	weng
sywan	hsüan	xuan	wo	wo	wo
sywe	hsüeh	xue	wu	wu	wu
sz	ssu, szu	si			
			ya	ya	ya
ta	t'a	ta	yai	yai	yai
tai	t'ai	tai	yan	yen	yan
tan	t'an	tan	yang	yang	yang
tang	t'ang	tang	yau	yao	yao
tau	t'ao	tao	ye	yeh	ye
te	t'e	te	yi	yi, i	yi
teng	t'eng	teng	yin	yin	yin
ti	t'i	ti	ying	ying	ying
ting	t'ing	ting	you	yu	you
tou	t'ou	tou	yu	yü	yu
tsa	ts'a	ca	yun	yün	yun
tsai	ts'ai	cai	yung	yung	yong
tsan	ts'an	can	ywan	yüan	yuan
tsang	ts'ang	cang	ywe	yüeh	yue